IT'S TIME

CELEBRATING
MATHS WITH PROJECTS

JENI WILSON AND LYNDA CUTTING

Heinemann
Portsmouth, NH

Dedication
To Sam, whose continued help has meant that this book
was finished in just twice as long

Heinemann
361 Hanover Street
Portsmouth, NH 03801-3912
A Division of Reed Publishing (USA), Inc.
Offices and agents throughout the world

First published 1991 in Australia by Oxford University Press
First published 1993 in the United States by Heinemann
ISBN 0-435-08791-6 (Heinemann)

Library of Congress Cataloging-in-Publication Data
Wilson, Jeni.
       It's time : celebrating maths with projects / Jeni Wilson and Lynda
Cutting.
       p. cm.
       Originally published : Melbourne : Oxford University Press, 1991.
       Includes bibliographical references.
       ISBN 0-435-08344-9
       1. Mathematics—Study and teaching (Primary) 2. Project method
in teaching. I. Cutting, Lynda. II. Title.
QA135.5.W498 1993   93-36421
372.7'044—dc20   CIP

Designed by Steve Randles
Typeset by Abb-Typesetting Pty Ltd, Collingwood, Victoria
Printed in the United States of America on Acid Free Paper
99 98 97 96 95 94 93 CC 1 2 3 4 5 6 7

Contents

INTRODUCTION

During the last few years there has been an increased interest in mathematics education which can be likened to the movement towards whole language programs of more than ten years ago.

Traditionally, components of language — spelling, reading, writing, listening and speaking — were taught in isolation. As knowledge of how children learn increased and the importance of whole language learning became understood teachers have been able to design programs that enabled children to utilise and develop their language skills in meaningful ways.

Many current educational documents emphasise:
- actively involving students in their own learning
- building on students' experiences and interests
- linking theory to practice
- fostering communication and co-operative learning
- encouraging risk-taking and learning from errors.

These principles have generally been accepted in the teaching of language yet warily, if at all, put into practice in mathematics programs.

The desire to apply our understandings to our mathematics programs (as we have done with language) has been hindered by many factors, including:
- the public perception of mathematics and pressure from parents, the general community, administrators and even other teachers;
- the lack of teacher confidence in the area of mathematics; and
- teachers' concern for covering externally imposed, structured and sequenced curriculum.

Teachers interested in this approach to mathematics commonly show concern about a number of issues, such as:
- Are students' maths skills being developed?
- Are students making the most of their time?
- Are the things they are doing challenging and worthwhile?

Much the same questions were once asked about using a conference approach to reading and writing, and in fact about any program that encourages students to take responsibility for their own learning.

We wholeheartedly believe that with careful planning, monitoring and record-keeping the answer to all these questions is yes! The same principles apply to the teaching and learning of maths as to any other subject.

As with other programs where students select their own topics and negotiate the scope and direction of their study there are times when some students appear to be making poor use of their time. Despite these occasional frustrations we would not consider discontinuing Maths Project time. Apart from the philosophical reasons for our using this approach to mathematics, our students wouldn't let us stop!

To experience a Maths Project session can be very exciting. Our Year 4 students were calculating square numbers in the thousands and a Year 3 student researched the history of maths from a book borrowed from the local library. Year 3 and 4 students were not only *doing* these things but *wanting* to do them. What is even more amazing is that students actually request to continue their work during their recess time!

As teachers we know the value of a positive attitude to learning and self-esteem. In our classroom we found that by using this approach to mathematics learning students' confidence increased, not only in mathematics but in all aspects of their school work.

Although we chose to call this book '*It's Time — Celebrating Maths with Projects*' this approach is not merely doing 'projects'; it involves many things, including establishing a supportive climate and predictable routines, trusting children to take responsibility for their own learning and expecting that they will. It involves conferencing and monitoring students' progress.

In summary, we advocate that teachers 'have a go' at using this approach to mathematics. In doing so they can begin to align their understandings of how children learn and the way they are teaching language with their mathematics programs. Given time you, too, will be able to join in the 'celebrations' during maths time.

Maths is easy when you only have to find the answer . . . the hard part is finding the question.

David, Year 1

1

••••••••••••••••••••••••••••••••

PLANNING AND ORGANISATION

Weekly planning

There is no recipe for planning the perfect maths program — there are, however, many strategies that can be used successfully which include: maths projects, integrated activities and activity maths, etc. These are usually used in combination, depending on the teacher's familiarity and degree of comfort with each and what is most appropriate at a specific time.

When planning a balanced maths program you need to consider many facets of program organisation such as:

- grouping arrangements;
- the use of varied materials/resources;
- including 'technology' studies;
- promoting discussion;
- including problem solving;
- allowing for individual differences in learning such as abilities, interests, pace and style;
- encouraging risk-taking, approximations and learning from errors; and
- the involvement of girls in the maths program.

Specific lesson planning must also be:

- balanced;
- enjoyable;
- challenging;
- meaningful;
- relevant;
- practical; and
- open-ended.

Example of a weekly plan for Year 3/4

Classroom topic: **Media**
Maths Focus: **Place value**

Monday	Tuesday	Wednesday
Media Quick Q's e.g. If there are 6 minutes of ads in a 30 min. program, how much of the show do you get to watch?	10 Quick Mixed 9's	Game: 'Place Value Bingo'
Read : The Hilton Hen House by Jo Hinchcliff. Discuss: What things did the farmer need to consider when rebuilding ?	Brainstorm + list : 'Where do we find Maths in the newspaper?'	Teach new place value game 'Magic 9's'
INTEGRATED Find the real estate section in the newspaper. You have a budget of b/w $150,000-180,000 + a family of four. Agree upon the most appropriate purchase. List reasons for your choice (choose a reporter scribe timekeeper + encourager)	ACTIVITIES Work out how much of a selected newspaper page is made up of ads. - Record your findings to share.	MATHS PROJECTS * Plan, start or continue projects Place Value Workshop • Jean • Keith • Marilyn • Phil share • Fiona (House design) • Sean/Craig (Fraction dominoes) • Alex (estimation)

Integrating literature with the classroom topic

Co-operative group activity

Problem-solving activity

Thursday	Friday
Mad minute	Tables Race
Play 'Magic 9's' (student as leader)	DISCUSSION Revise when & how to publish LIST ideas for publishing
MATHS * Plan, start projects Fractions Workshop • Kath • Jo • Marco • Ali Share • David & Kerryn (Plan only) • Hayley (2nd draft of ads in newspaper problem)	PROJECTS or continue Publishing Workshop (on demand) Conference • Yve • Greg • Colin • Leonie Share • Stephen (tables patterns) • Sally (finished model) • Danni & Clinton (tape recording— Maths opinion survey)

Quick Maths
• automatic response
• number facts
5–15 minutes
} Whole class

Introductory activity
5–15 minutes
} Whole class

Activity time

Workshops
20–40 minutes
} Individual and small group work

Share time
5–15 minutes
} Whole class

There may be occasions when you would continue an activity or devote extra time to class investigations instead of doing 'Maths Projects'. However, while the content of the week may vary the basic routine would, on the whole, be virtually the same each week.

Weekly organisation

Maths projects are one component of my maths program. By setting up independent activities I can spend concentrated time working with a small group of students on their projects, I know then that I will see every kid every week. After kids finish their tasks they can go on with their projects — they look forward to doing this.

My daily program is predictable; it includes the following:

Figure 1.1   An example of a teacher's weekly program plans

Quick Maths
 	
- number between __ + __
- 3 more than
- addition
	Group Activities (rotating)
	
	1. Pascal's triangle - addition
	   Add numbers to complete
	   (may use calculator).
	
	2. Counting large numbers of things
	   Develop strategies
	
	3. Length - measure (after estimating the length of a piece of wool stuck on a card)

Whole Class Activities • Flip, slip, Turn - (TV prog) - triangles/ triangular numbers. • Maths Break - counting large number (TV) of things • Discuss Pascal's triangle	

- Quick Maths
- Whole class
  modelling
  integrating
- Small group activities
  Maths Projects
  open-ended problems
  co-operative group work
  estimation
- Share time

The start of every maths session begins with Quick Maths. I keep a record of my Quick Maths (mental arithmetic) in an exercise book to look back to see if we've changed and progressed. The kids also keep their answers in their own exercise book.

Then we have a whole class session which usually lasts between 5–20 minutes depending on what we are doing. If appropriate I integrate the social ed topic, but if it is going to be contrived I choose something else, for example: when studying the environment we measured a walking track, did mapping and worked out scale. If the topic is not appropriate we would look at an area that had been neglected, e.g. mass, calculators etc. On Mondays much of this whole class time is spent explaining the group activities.

After the whole class time students work on small activities (in mixed groups of gender, ethnic background and ability). The activities have been prepared and listed on a chart. On the first day I set up all the activities but on the following days kids do this themselves. During the week every group experiences every activity.

About two to three times a week we have a share time. I encourage those who are keen and others who have made interesting discoveries to share. I also ask particular kids to share their work so that everyone gets a turn. To ensure this I keep a class list of 'sharers'.

Andrea Johnson
Lalor Primary School

I think it's much better to work in groups because you get a lot of ideas and it's just easier.

Cain, Year 3

Daily Organisation

Figure 1.2 is an example of a daily routine that can be used at any Year level. This format is suggested as it includes all elements of a balanced mathematics program.

Figure 1.2 An example of a daily routine

Quick maths

e.g.: • automatic response
- number facts
- tables
- counting, pattern and order

(5–15 minutes)

Game/introduce new idea/activity

e.g.: • place value
- use of literature
- thematic problem

Ideas may be taken up by students for further investigation.

(5–15 minutes)

Independent activity time

- student/teacher initiated projects
- activities
- planned lesson/concept development (whole class or small teaching groups)

Workshops:
- similar to clinic groups in reading and writing
- groups meet to discuss, practise, revise ideas, concepts etc.
- these can be voluntary or selected by the teacher; with experience children can run these themselves.

Conferences
- voluntary or on demand
- individual or group

(20–40 minutes)

**Share/reflection time
(student request or teacher chosen)**

- celebrate successes
- share processes and problems
- ask for help or give suggestions

(5–15 minutes)

Developing a co-operative working environment

To enable all class members to get maximum benefit from this approach to maths it is important to develop an atmosphere in which students feel confident to take risks, to actively share their ideas and to learn with each other.

This sounds very simple, but in practice much time is needed to develop the skills involved and to help students understand the importance of working together.

I reckon it's easier to work in groups because you've got more brains and then it's easier.

Amanda, Year 3

A group of students working independently of the teacher.

Development of co-operative group skills is both important in the general curriculum and valuable when encouraging students to work independently of the teacher. This independence allows the teacher to hold workshop sessions and conferences with a minimum of interruption and encourages students to use each other as a resource. See Co-operative learning skills checklist on page 96.

The teacher's role

In a co-operative, problem-solving approach to mathematics learning the teacher encourages students to be interdependent, to ask questions and help each other before coming to him/her, to collect and share materials and to assess their own skills. Though no less important, the teacher's role is one of facilitator or manager. In that role the teacher will need to:

● provide clear guidelines and expectations;

I like doing Maths Projects 'cause you get to change maths into a project and you can choose what you want to do. I learnt how to make measurements — you know, how to rule up. I learnt how to do addition and subtraction — it's easier than it ever was before.

Paul, Year 4

- establish predictable routines, for example: what to do if the teacher is busy and what to do when finished;
- be available but not too easily accessible;
- model appropriate behaviour, for example, be encouraging and enthusiastic;
- highlight the importance and value of working together;
- gauge progress;

- lead discussions and teach necessary skills;
- give students positive and appropriate feedback;
- provide time for students to share their problems and successes;
- organise the physical environment: create space for individual, small group and whole class activities;
- involve students in their own assessment; and
- make time for activities based on students' interests and needs that practise, revise and reinforce skills.

In addition to all these managerial issues there is still a need to 'teach' and model skills, concepts and strategies. For example, how to solve problems, how to collect and represent data. Teachers need to make their processes and actions explicit. For example, though there may be more than one possible strategy, one may be more efficient.

Teachers must therefore have a clear understanding of mathematics expectations and processes to ensure worthwhile conferencing and reflection.

As well as being a 'facilitator' the teacher still needs to teach and model skills.

You get more done and if you don't know something you can just ask your partner.

Danielle, Year 4

I like Maths Projects, it is better than proper maths. It is fun because you can ask other people's opinions and you can do it in groups. When I did one on counting I learnt ways of counting in different languages. I also did one on architecture with two other friends. We tried to make a house out of icy-pole sticks but realised it was too hard. The arches didn't work. We learnt a lot about building by going to the library.

Simone, Year 6

Students building an aviary for Houdini.

Maths Projects in a multi-aged grade

This year I team teach in a Year 3, 4, 5, 6 multi-age classroom. Maths Projects works just as effectively for us as it does in other grade structures. Children in a multi-age classroom situation develop positive social skills that I believe are necessary to run a successful Maths Project program, for example:

- a strong sense of community spirit through interaction with others;
- responsible attitudes and tolerance towards others; and
- co-operative skills.

Before branching into Maths Projects we spent some time developing co-operative group skills. We also established very firm and comprehensive guidelines about the process and procedures. In many ways this approach is very similar to process writing.

If children are unsure of the process, or certain stages are left out, problems can arise; for example if a child wishes to build a model and rushes into the construction without planning and organising materials in advance. The same applies if we are not well organised. This includes keeping on-going records, giving students a timeline and providing input when it is needed.

Some of the positive advantages that we have observed during Maths Projects are:

- children participate in peer coaching;
- children work at their own level;
- they attempt challenging topics (some of our class built a bird aviary for the pet galah; they had to plan, measure angles, cost materials etc.);
- low achievers find success and this builds their self-esteem;
- projects are usually related to real life situations; and
- there is a high level of interest because children are allowed to make their own choices.

Margaret Smith
Greenbrook Primary School

**Teaching points/
strategies**

Integrating maths with the ▶
social education topic

Using the library as a ▶
resource

Using maths in real life ▶
problem-solving
situations

Students solving their own
problems ▶

Students learning
co-operatively ▶

Mathematical skills —
measurement ▶

Students talking to solve
problems ▶

Learning from errors ▶

Building on confidence/
sharing successes ▶

Making connections and
extending knowledge ▶

Example of a co-operative Year 3 and 4 group project — making soft toys

During our Year 3 and 4 camp to Phillip Island we made a trip to see the penguins. A number of the children found they couldn't afford to buy the souvenir penguin they wanted. I suggested that when we got back to school they could make one.

When we arrived back at school we went to the library to find some resources. We finally found a pattern for a toy penguin in an old book. The problem was that they had to draft their own pattern.

Drafting the pattern — 'no problem' they bragged — but in fact it set them many challenges. First they realised they would have to decide the size of the finished penguin and consequently the ratio to which they had to enlarge the grid squares. (This was largely determined by the size of the piece of black fabric they had found.)

Eventually they decided on 4 cm grid squares. They got the largest piece of paper they could find and set about marking out their grid. Michael quickly calculated that if each square was 4 cm their paper wasn't going to be big enough for all the squares required. There was a lot of animated discussion and finally the group conceded that Michael's logic (supported by a calculator) was right. They decided that if they worked in pairs and joined their papers together everything would fit in and they could share the finished pattern.

'Counting by fours' to mark the grids 'is easy' they commented, but they soon found out that even one error meant they had to start all over again.

They even found that ruling straight lines from point to point wasn't so easy, especially when your paper was over 50 cm long and your ruler was only 30 cm.

After more group discussion they eventually solved this problem too. Another row of dots measured along the middle helped the process of getting the squares ruled and numbered.

The next issue was whether to number the spaces or the lines. This time Jason insisted that it didn't matter as long as they numbered their grids and the pattern the same way. The other group members went along with this and fortunately Jason proved to be correct.

During working time I observed a lot of drawing, talking, rubbing out and even, occasionally, quiet cursing. During the third session the pattern was completed, pinned onto their fabric and cut out. Following the pattern's instructions the penguins were sewn together (with a little bit of help from a mum with a sewing machine).

They were very proud of themselves when they presented their penguins to the class and they carefully explained how they had gone about their project.

Their penguins were displayed and played with for much of the year, but this was not the end of it. Realising that if you could enlarge with grids you could also reduce, they enlarged and reduced a number of complicated pictures and shapes. This extended to an investigation of 'ratio'. For example, when asked they knew that if you double the size of the grid you double the size of the finished shape.

Two of the boys went on to look at other uses of grids such as map reading, street directories and, in an atlas, using longitude and latitude.

Jason and Michael became so interested in sewing that they tried it again using a different sort of pattern. This time they had to follow more complicated instructions. For example, 'to make the head cut out a circle with a radius of 10 cm'. The amount of geometric information they got out of this was incredible.

After they had been working on their projects for about a month I asked them to list down what they had learnt. We were all amazed!

THINGS WE LEARNT.
- Used grids to enlarge things.
- Measuring long lines with little rulers.
- To be careful when we counted by 4's
- Its easier when you join your work with someone else
- That if you can make things bigger with grids you can also make them smaller too.
- If you double the size of the squares you double the size of the shape.
- You can copy a picture with grids.
- We had to double to work out how much material.
- You have to read the instructions carefully.
- You should listen to everyone's ideas.

Use of commercially published materials/schemes

There is a wide variety of commercially produced maths resources. If your school has invested in a scheme use it like other books and materials — as a resource when it is relevant to your students' needs.

Some materials in schemes are classified according to specific or isolated content, for example fractions, place value or area. This material could be useful for ideas for introductory activities or workshops.

This material may even be made available for student selection: for example, refer students to certain books, materials etc. or use it during conferences when discussing new topics.

Teachers should familiarise themselves with what is available and then use the resources within an integrated and balanced program.

If you get stuck someone can help you.
Kevin, Year 4

2

• •

Teachers' Questions Answered

Don't students waste time?
• •

We have never found this to be a great problem. In fact we have found just the opposite. Because students have chosen what they are investigating their interest is high and their enthusiasm and effort great.

If in the beginning students are having difficulty getting started call a workshop or encourage them to talk to others about ideas. Once students start sharing plans and projects enthusiasm seems to rub off; the problem then will be to get them to pack up!

Isn't it just for older students?
• •

No. Even Preps can participate in a Conference approach to maths. With younger students the teacher has more of the responsibility to:
- be available to act as scribe as necessary;
- keep up the daily activity records (some students will be able to assist you with this by dating their own scrap book/folder, or you could appoint a date-stamp monitor);
- ensure that a wide variety of materials are clearly labelled and easily accessible;
- continually model the uses of concrete materials; and
- understand that projects may not necessarily be long term or ongoing.

Even the youngest students enjoy doing Maths Projects. Given the choice and materials we have seen Year 1 students discover patterns on the calculator and practise copious division sums . . . things inconceivable in a traditional maths program.

Continual modelling of the uses of concrete materials is vital with younger students.

How long can students work on one project?

This will depend on the age of the students and the amount of time you devote to Project Maths. If your time allowance is two sessions per week you might decide three weeks is long enough for Year 4 students to spend working on one idea.

During the early stages establish clear ground rules, but be prepared to negotiate with individuals. As a teacher you know your students and you are the best one to decide if more or less time is needed.

What if students do the same thing all the time?

Initially this could be a problem. If students are unfamiliar with taking responsibility for their own learning, lack confidence or have few ideas to work on you will need to model varied and stimulating ideas. This can be done during the introductory sessions, in other maths times or incidentally. Workshops and share times are another source of ideas for students.

A good way to start the approach is to brainstorm 'What maths is . . .' then ask students what they would like to explore. Ideas can be listed on charts and/or in their folders. This list can also be used to help gauge the balance of the maths program.

A student brain-storming a new maths topic. He uses teachers' guides for reference.

Another way to ensure that children are not constantly covering the same ground is the requirement that they keep a record of their daily activities (see page 20). Sharing, setting expectations and celebrating students' achievements will promote confidence and provide a springboard for more adventurous and challenging projects.

How do I know if students are learning?

Some teachers feel that if they are not teaching in the traditional manner then their students are not learning. This is simply not true.

When using a conference approach to reading, writing or maths it is essential to keep good records to see results for yourself and to justify the approach to others if necessary.

Students can help you with this task. You will need to constantly remind them and check that they are keeping their records of daily activities. You, too, can add comments to these of your observations during workshops or roving conferences (see figure 2.1 over the page).

Although we do not approve of tests for their own sake we have used diagnostic tests designed and used for the specific purpose of gauging children's progress and establishing areas of difficulty. The results of these tests certainly put our minds at rest.

The pleasing thing is that not only do students do well on these formal tests they also achieve in areas that are difficult to test, such as problem solving, co-operative learning skills and confidence.

Figure 2.1 An example of comments made by both the student and the teacher in a student's record of his daily activities

Name:	*David Baxter*	
Date	*Activity*	*Conference*
20/2	comparing old time measurement	• FROM CLASS INTRO. • SUGGEST YOU CHECK ON A CALCULATOR • ENTHUSIASTIC

I know what my kids should know in reading and writing but how do I know what they should know in maths?

This is probably one of the major reasons why teachers have, in the past, been reluctant to allow their students the same independence and responsibility in maths as they have in their language programs.

This is especially ironic since one of the greatest pluses of this approach is that students are actually more enthusiastic about maths because they are allowed to explore what interests them.

Unfortunately, teachers may feel that they are not in control — this of course is not true. The role of the teacher is an important one. They are still required to ensure that students learn skills and concepts but this is done in a different way and at times when it is relevant, such as in introductory sessions, workshops and share times. See pages 8 to 12.

The course content is still determined by curriculum documents and by school policy and programs. It is through the use of such documents and commercially produced material that we can educate ourselves. We need to become familiar with curriculum expectations and our students' needs.

Because this approach encourages a broad range of (often integrated) concepts and strategies you will need to draw upon a variety of resources. One idea is to establish a list of concepts and strategies you want to cover over the year (see Chapter 6 and page 94) and use this not only during your evaluation but as an aid to your planning. Mark off the areas covered then you can satisfy yourself that you are providing your students with a balanced program.

How do I make sure I cover everything?

It is very important to make yourself aware of the required mathematics objectives (see pages 94 and 95 for record keeping examples). Your work program is then a record of your introductory sessions, workshops and other experiences. This enables you to look back over what you have already done. Some teachers assess the balance of their programs at the end of each week, month, unit or term, then address any issues they have neglected. Some areas may only need to be covered in small group activities.

If the students are writing all the time how do they get time to do any maths?

This question reveals a misconception of a conference approach to maths, probably originating from the perceived connection to 'process writing'.

Some projects do involve recording findings but the exploration of ideas and concrete materials is of more importance. If discoveries are then to be represented or recorded this can be done in a variety of ways, for example as models, photos or in writing.

Figure 2.2   A representation of the process of most investigations

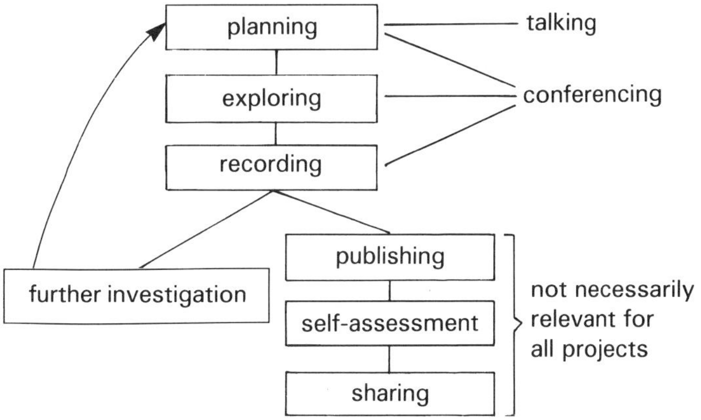

Talking, sharing and conferencing are a very important part of the process but the value of recording findings should not be underestimated. Making a record of their work helps students to clarify their ideas. Doing it is one thing but writing about it and explaining it is yet another!

There is no denying that writing has a place in this approach to mathematics but it is only one part of the process. The degree to which students write during their investigations will vary according to their age and particular study. For example, research into the history of Numeration Systems will involve a lot of written work, designing a birdcage will be best represented diagrammatically, and the results of a survey could be best shown on a graph. The teacher can decide how often he/she wants a written report on the projects. This might vary from a report on every project to once a term.

Where do computers and calculators fit in?

Like pens, computers and calculators are tools. Ideally, they would be readily available for students to use in their projects as necessary but teachers know that this is not always possible. Try a roster system to ensure that students have access to these at least one Maths Projects session per week. At times you may also like to teach certain computer/calculator skills during introductory or workshop sessions.

This student is using a pocket calculator to help him with his maths project.

A parent's view

As I walked around the classroom I heard snippets of conversations, things like:

Do you want to work with me?
What will we do?
Where will we get our information?
Maybe we could . . . ?
What equipment do we need?

I thought the classroom was noisy, but the children were all busy and enthusiastic about what they were doing. The children were getting chances to try out their ideas and theories. It was great to see them working co-operatively.

Linda Dunn

3

GETTING STARTED

Some people seem to be under the impression that getting organised for this approach is very time consuming and difficult. We disagree.

For Project Maths sessions to run efficiently from the outset some preparation will, of course, be required. The actual sessions from then on will require no more organisation than any other mathematics lessons. Students themselves can assist with the organisation of materials and later even be workshop session leaders.

Here are some suggestions to help your program run as smoothly as possible (in rough order of urgency).

1 *Purchase one folder for each student.* This could take a variety of forms: a scrap book for infants, a manilla folder, an exercise book or an art folio (plastic or cardboard) for older students. Figure 3.1 shows how we organise the folders in our Year 3/4 class.

2 *Collect and display resources.* These could include books, curriculum guides, concrete materials, games and student-made materials.

Make sure these are clearly labelled and easily accessible. Use trolley tubs, a filing system or cardboard boxes.

3 *Acquire some major equipment.* Essential to the smooth running of the program is either a whiteboard or a blackboard and large sheets of cheap paper.

Other invaluable equipment: an overhead projector and a flannelboard. Send home a note to ask for donations of discrete materials.

4 *Inform people about this approach.* Let other teachers, parents and, most importantly, your students know what you are planning. Some students will have little experience with taking responsibility for their own learning so it is important to establish clear ground rules and routines.

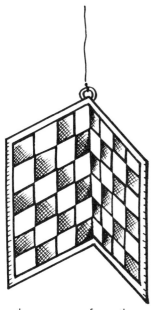
hang games from the roof

Figure 3.1 Each student records their Project Maths activities and progress in a folder

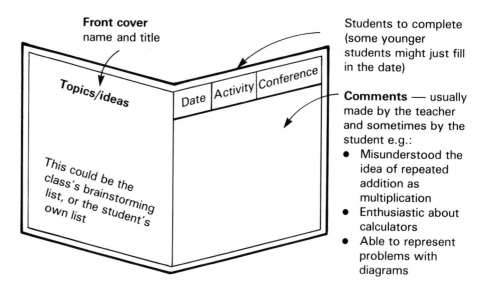

Front cover
name and title

Topics/ideas

This could be the class's brainstorming list, or the student's own list

Date | Activity | Conference

Students to complete (some younger students might just fill in the date)

Comments — usually made by the teacher and sometimes by the student e.g.:
● Misunderstood the idea of repeated addition as multiplication
● Enthusiastic about calculators
● Able to represent problems with diagrams

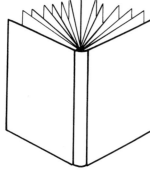

cards stored in plastic sleeves

loose-leaf folder

Explain to them why you think it is a good approach, how it can be enjoyable for everyone and compare the routine to that of your language program. Emphasise the importance of the students participating by:

● keeping their own records;

● planning for themselves; and

● evaluating their own work.

At this stage there are a number of ways to actually start students working in this manner.

● Spend some time developing a co-operative working climate within your classroom.

Things we can do and say to work well together
● say 'that was good'
● say 'thank you'
● share ideas
● listen
● help other people
● co-operate
● use quiet voices
● take turns
● speak up
● encourage people

- Brainstorm 'What is maths?' then use the list as a source of possible topics.

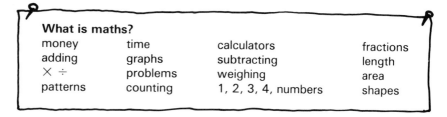

What is maths?

money	time	calculators	fractions
adding	graphs	subtracting	length
× ÷	problems	weighing	area
patterns	counting	1, 2, 3, 4, numbers	shapes

- Choose one topic (possibly from the list) for all students to investigate. This may be the easiest way to start but be cautious; some students may resent having to 'do' a project they have no interest in. Their efforts may not be a true reflection of their capabilities.

- Simply let students choose any topic and capitalise on successes and problems as they arise — this can be overwhelming for some students and teachers. WARNING: don't expect to be able to conference every student in the first week.

- Do mini-lessons as preparation. For example:
  - The whole class does a problem-solving activity then completes a self-evaluation form on their performance.

  - Brainstorm a topic together then ask students to take one aspect to plan further with others.

- Do mathematical activities such as RIME (Reality in Maths Education) that require a written response.

- Model the process of doing a maths project yourself by going through the routine of planning, exploring, talking, sharing, recording, presenting and self-assessment.

6 After you have given students some time working together, planning and evaluating, *take time to chat about ideas and presentation methods.* Make lists for display to serve as reminders which can be periodically revised.

7 *Share projects with other Years and schools.* This is another way of valuing students' work and providing ideas for others.

8 *Share your ideas, successes and frustrations with your peers.* This will help *you.*

A student sharing his work with the whole class.

Ways to present projects
- posters
- tape recordings
- models
- drawings or diagrams
- books
- games
- activity sheets for the class
- mobiles

Why and how we started

We were highly motivated to start Project Maths. Our enthusiasm seemed to bubble over to the children. We had already developed a co-operative environment in the room and were using co-operative group work in all curriculum areas. This kind of environment is ideal, probably a pre-requisite, for this approach.

We began with a simple question: What is Maths? The children were asked to write, draw or concept map their responses to be displayed. A list of pure and applied mathematical areas of possible study was derived from their work.

We also brainstormed other topics as a whole class group. The children then made individual lists in the back of their Project Maths books of ideas they would like to investigate. We showed and displayed samples of work produced from other schools. We also conducted some cross-age tutoring sessions to offer support to and encourage team planning amongst the staff. These sessions enhanced the co-operative skills of both younger and older children.

The children are developing a variety of skills and concepts. Maths is more meaningful when integrated into the curriculum, because it is real life. Our children are more motivated in mathematics-related activities. Surprisingly, they are now actually asking 'When are we doing Maths?'.

Carmela Bianco and Andrew Merryweather
Greenbrook Primary School

Classroom organisation — getting started

Kids need help getting started — they don't 'just do it'. Prior to starting Maths Projects we spend a lot of time working through many teacher-directed activities, for example: 'What is your name worth?'. Children may later wish to extend these ideas — 'What is your friend/ parent/teacher/pet's name worth?' etc. or further develop these into their own Maths Projects. I write these activity ideas onto cards which are stored in a Maths Ideas Box. Children have access to the cards as a source of topic ideas. Many of the ideas are from FAMPA (Family and Mathematics Project Australia), commercially produced books, childrens literature, and from the children. These are collected during share time when children discuss their work. The class is encouraged to ask questions and may add their own thoughts about how to further develop the idea.

This getting ready time can last for weeks. When we start Maths Projects I set aside a specific time for project work each week, however this is not my complete Maths program. During the project sessions we always begin with a ten minute activity; either an open-ended problem, or children sharing their work at various stages of completion.

Children enjoy the opportunity to work at their own pace on something that interests them. Sometimes when they work on a project they learn things that I would never anticipate, let alone plan. It is very rewarding when children make discoveries themselves and when they are excited about sharing them.

Ingrid Wilson
Greenbrook Primary School

Example of a start of the year maths lesson (Year 4)

Teaching points/ strategies

INTRODUCTORY
ACTIVITY ▶
Gauging students'
understandings ▶

Building on students'
interests ▶

Involving students
physically in a high
interest activity ▶

WORKING/ACTIVITY
TIME ▶

This approach was new to the teacher but she was enthusiastic to try it. As an introduction she decided to brainstorm with the whole class 'What is maths?' (see page 21). She was surprised to find that students had so many ideas.

She had planned to simply decorate covers and copy the list of possible topics onto their folders, but an idea came up that she decided to capitalise on. One of the students suggested that estimation should go onto the list. The teacher gave an example of how she needed to estimate whether she had enough petrol to get to school that morning. Then she picked up a ruler and asked students to estimate how far it would drop before they could catch it. Students made a note of their estimations and a volunteer came out to the front to try it. She held the ruler and the student held her fingers open at zero. The ruler was dropped and recaptured at 10 cm. Not a bad reaction time for the first try. Students were then allowed to try this in pairs.

After a few minutes the teacher stopped the activity to explain the format of the session. Students could either:

- further explore the reaction time/ruler activity then write a report about it;

**Teaching points/
strategies**

Students responsible for ▶
their own record
keeping

Students learning ▶
co-operatively

Time for the teacher to
observe, take notes and
respond to the interests
of students ▶

CONFERENCE ▶

Asking questions to have ▶
students verbalise
understandings

SHARE TIME ▶

Allowing students time to
reflect on their work ▶

Involving students in
self-assessment ▶
Informing students about ▶
predictable procedures

- use the Brainstorm List to plan a project;
- write all they knew about any maths concept; or
- meet on the floor if they were unsure of what to do or for a workshop if needed.

The teacher then reminded students to note the date and their activity in their Maths Project book.

Most students were eager to start. Some kept going with the introductory activity. Some wrote while two groups formed to work together, one chose a scribe (without knowing the terminology) to record the estimated length of the classroom pet lizard and three students remained on the floor. The teacher encouraged the students to talk about their own examples of ideas on the class list, and their own interests. She told them that she could not decide what they should investigate for them and that they might like to have a look at what the others were doing. It wasn't long before all students were very much involved in their own projects. The teacher was able to spend some time observing and talking to students about their plans and, work.

The amount of actual mathematical content varied between students and groups. The lizard group soon asked for a conference. The teacher said little while group members picked up other's errors. She asked a few mathematical questions in relation to length, for example, 'How much bigger is Houdini than Aristotle?' (classroom pets). She noted the names of some students who might need to attend a workshop at a later date.

After about half an hour the teacher warned that there was only about five minutes to go.

There were plenty of students willing to share their projects. The ideas were indeed varied. These were to provide a valuable source of inspiration to others in subsequent project time.

Just before it was time for lunch the teacher asked her students to reflect upon:

- what they had learnt, and
- what they liked or disliked.

She asked them to jot their notes down on a piece of paper and told the class 'whenever we do Project Maths I will expect you to think about what you have done.'

4

INTRODUCTORY ACTIVITIES

What are introductory activities and why do we need them?

I don't like maths off the board. In Maths Projects you get to choose what you want to do, like: time, measuring or money around the world.

Daniel, Year 4

The Maths Project approach to mathematics allows children to not only find the answers but also to formulate their own questions. For children to be able to do this they need to be exposed to a wide variety of mathematical ideas, skills and concepts.

This is the main purpose of the introductory session. The teacher (or sometimes a student) plans and prepares a short teaching session aimed at expanding children's general mathematical understandings and giving them a broader range of options for their own projects. It is also an opportunity to discuss and model strategies such as planning, gathering data and presenting information in the most appropriate way. One way to finish an introductory session is to say 'You can use these ideas or continue your own projects'.

Daily introductory sessions should be planned to allow time to teach specific skills or develop understandings. They should be based on observations of what needs to be covered by the whole Year. By actively involving children in demonstrations they can see that there are a variety of ways to approach any given task. Finally, the introductory session 'sets the scene' for the work that follows by helping to build a positive working environment and create a feeling of a 'maths community' within the class.

The length of time devoted to these sessions should generally be between ten and twenty minutes but this will vary according to the Year levels and on the content being discussed.

The range of activities that can be undertaken is endless; for example, the activity might include literature or other thematic activities. A selection of Introductory Activity ideas for content areas is given in chapter 7. Although these are divided into maths topics for convenience, ideally they would be taught in meaningful contexts, that is, where they relate to the current class theme or to meet specific class needs. An example which illustrates how an introductory activity has led to an independent project and workshop follows.

An example of how an introductory session led to a maths project

As 'Time' had only been dealt with incidently during the year and no one had investigated this area in their projects we decided to base our introductory session on this area.

'How long is a minute?' was the first question we asked. How long it seems when you're silent for that length of time! 'How many times can you clap in one minute?' Students' guesses were listed on a chart and then we clapped for that length of time (watch out for clappers shrewd enough to slow down or speed up to suit their guess). Because of the excitement we extended this activity for one or two minutes, revising, doubling and halving.

Figure 4.1 An example of a draft project on Time which was initiated as a result of an introductory session

5

INDEPENDENT ACTIVITY TIME

The Routine

After the class has worked together during the introductory session the students move off to work on their projects, either as individuals, in pairs or in small groups. Students collect their folders and any equipment they feel they need. For movement to be smooth (and relatively quiet) students should be given responsibility for the collection and storage of their own equipment. Naturally they must have easy access to all resources.

There is a need to continually stress the importance of students helping each other. This will improve as students develop co-operative group skills. During this time the teachers walk around

A permanent heading on a small blackboard is used here to organise conference bookings. Students fill in their names when they want a conference; in that way the teacher can see them in order.

observing and conferencing students as needed; this is especially important while students are getting used to the routine.

Once students are involved in their projects (usually after five minutes) teachers meet with the workshop group. When these workshops are completed conferences are continued, either individual or group, student- or teacher-initiated. It is important to realise that there will not be time to have prolonged conferences or workshops with every student every week. This is a valuable time in which to talk, assess and be a part of each student's struggles and successes.

Workshops

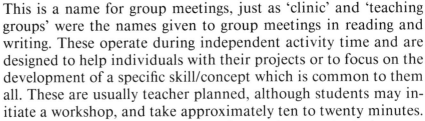

This is a name for group meetings, just as 'clinic' and 'teaching groups' were the names given to group meetings in reading and writing. These operate during independent activity time and are designed to help individuals with their projects or to focus on the development of a specific skill/concept which is common to them all. These are usually teacher planned, although students may initiate a workshop, and take approximately ten to twenty minutes.

We play games in workshops.   **Sophia, Year 2**

Select the students based on observations made during conferences and activity times or, at the end of the introductory session, say, for example, 'We're having a workshop on working out the circumference of a circle. Who would be interested in taking part?'. Those who are interested then meet later in the workshop. It is surprising and pleasing that students are usually accurate at assessing their own needs. Usually the students who volunteered for a workshop are the ones the teacher would have identified him/herself.

The actual content of the workshops should be determined by the students' needs, as identified during assessment procedures.

Some students work independently while others take part in a workshop with the teacher.

They will often be concerned with skill and concept development or problem-solving strategies.

At the end of the lesson it is important to allow those who took part in the workshop time to share what they have learnt with the rest of the class.

<table>
<tr><td>

Teaching points/ strategies

▼

Integrating maths ▶

Workshop volunteers ▶

Non-threatening activity ▶

Allowing for individual abilities, pace, style etc. ▶

Recording in a variety of ways ▶

</td></tr>
</table>

Example of a Prep and Year 1/2 workshop with a literature focus

The class had been involved in the study of transportation. We had visited *Polly Woodside* and were looking at boats and ships. I asked if any children were interested in listening to me read one of their favourite stories *'Who Sank the Boat?'* by Pamela Allen. Four Prep, one Year 1 and one Year 2 students volunteered for the workshop. After we had read the story I asked them to represent what had happened in the book.

Two Preps, Andrew and Bevan, and Trevor from Year 2 used plasticine to make models of the animal characters and put them in a boat made from the top of an egg carton. They then retold the story to me using their models. I asked them to record what had happened so they wrote down exactly what they had said, 'the cow got in, the donkey got in' etc.

David from Year 1 stacked Unifix cubes which he used to represent the relative sizes of the animals.

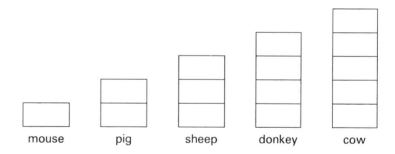

mouse   pig   sheep   donkey   cow

When asked to record his story he did so in picture form:

Sascha and Nellie, both from Prep, immediately started writing; they used tally marks to represent the characters.

Teacher as a resource ▶   Sascha asked, 'How do you write "and"?'. I replied, 'You know how to spell that.' 'No,' she replied, 'not like that — in maths writing!'

Students discovering for ▶ I realised they wanted the addition sign. When they completed their themselves   work they brought me an equation:

**Teaching points/
strategies**

▼

$$1 + 1 + 1 + 1 + 1 = 5$$

Students learning
co-operatively ▶

Peer-tutoring ▶

When I asked them to tell me about their work they explained that 'one got in and one more got in and one more and one more and one more and that equalled five in the boat.' I congratulated them on their work and having taught themselves to do 'plus' equations. 'Did we?' they asked, happily surprised, and went off to explain this to the rest of the group. The rest of the group very quickly started writing the same type of equations. David was the only exception. He explained that he could already do addition and he thought his diagrams were more interesting anyway.

Conferencing

I like conferences, the teacher doesn't say much but they help me anyway.
George, Year 5

During conferencing students get a chance to explain, justify and question. It is a time for teachers to offer support and guidance to students, and a chance to make evaluative observations and notes.

Roving, individual and group conferences are held during independent activity time.

The teacher conferences a student as the others get started. The student has her records easily accessible in her plastic pocket.

During conferencing, concepts and skills can be explored with individual students. Avoid correcting all errors in the first conference — focus on only two or three aspects of the project. It is also better to use activities (such as those listed in this book) to demonstrate strategies, rather than just telling the student the answer.

Work which the students publish should have errors (mathematical and language) corrected. The reason for this should be made explicit to students.

It is suggested that group conferences:
- be predictable — students know what to bring and what to expect;
- encourage student-initiated talk — students help each other and find solutions to their own problems;
- enable students to feel free to take risks and responsibility and therefore keep ownership of their own work;

In Maths Projects we learnt how to plan out our work. You don't usually do that sort of thing everyday. You can work together so you can share ideas and it's easier.

Lawren, Year 6

Student and teacher in an individual conference.

- pose questions which are open-ended (see p. 32 for generic questions);
- be short — students may wish to continue the conference after the teacher leaves the group;
- give encouraging and specific feedback; and
- be held in an area in sight of the rest of the class, but one that is slightly removed.

A group conference.

An example of a student initiated conference

Explanation/ background ▼		Conference ▼	Teaching point/ strategies ▼
After an introductory session Troy approaches the teacher, who had asked the class to reflect on their strengths and weaknesses as a source for new topics.	TROY	'I want to do something on fractions because I'm hopeless at them.'	
	TEACHER	'Have you got anything planned so far?'	◀ Question to gauge progress so far
Troy is a highly motivated student who rarely seeks assistance.	TROY	'No. I don't know where to start.'	
	TEACHER	'Have you had a look at the books and fraction tray on our trolley?'	◀ Remind student about resources available without giving specific directions
	TROY	'No I just thought about the idea.'	
	TEACHER	'How about starting with the Teacher's Guidelines to see if anything interests you?'	◀ Valuing the student's interests
	TROY	'O.K.'	
	TEACHER	'Come back if you don't get anywhere. You could talk to Craig and Kevin, they've just done a project on fractions.'	◀ Being an available resource ◀ Encouraging peer tutoring and sharing

Generic questions for conferencing

- Tell me/us about your project in one or two sentences?
- Where did you get the idea from?
- What have you planned to do?
- What resources do you think you will need?
- Have you talked to anyone about your ideas? Who? What suggestions did they make?
- What do you want to find out about?
- What have you found out so far?
- What is the next thing you are going to do?

FURTHER QUESTIONS

- What is one thing you liked/disliked about this project?
- What is the most interesting thing you have found out?
- How are you going to present this information?
- Could you use diagrams/graphs to present your findings?
- Do you have any recommendations for others doing a similar project?

6

• •

RECORD KEEPING AND ASSESSMENT

Student assessment

Assessment is the process of collecting information and making judgements about actions to improve learning. The use of a variety of assessment techniques is the best way to ensure an under-standing of all aspects of your students' progress. Select the most appropriate techniques according to your lesson's objectives. Make assessment an ongoing and integral part of your routine.

METHODS OF ASSESSMENT

Methods of assessment include:

1 **Observation.** The value of observation cannot be underestim-ated. Valuable observations can be made during 'roving' confer-ences, group conferences, workshops or share times.
2 **Anecdotal notes.** Record observations and other valuable in-formation on:
   - Class lists. In this way you can keep a check on students that might otherwise be 'forgotten'.
   - In students' workbooks (see p. 20). These can be completed by either the teacher or by the students themselves. Comments on attitude, group skills, problem-solving strategies and concept development should be included.
3 Keep **files** of students' work. Tell them why you do this and give them access to their own files. Make a point of going through these with each student at regular intervals so that you can both see the progress being made.

4 **Diagnostic comments.** These can be attached to students' work. Use checklists (see pages 96 and 97) to guide your comments. These will help you in your assessment and evaluation and can be used to demonstrate progress to parents and co-ordinators.

5 Ask students to **assess themselves**. These self-assessments can then be added to their files (some proformas have been included on pages 91, 92 and 93). They can be used after specific topics or after a number of weeks.

6 **Tests** can also be a valuable assessment technique if they are diagnostic, for a specific purpose and the information gathered is then used for further reference. Students might even design their own tests and worksheets.

7 You might also ask students to keep a **journal**. This could be specifically about mathematics learning or school life in general.

Program evaluation

It is the teacher's responsibility to provide his/her students with an effective, balanced mathematics program. Good record keeping is therefore vital.

A number of the methods used to assess students' progress can also be helpful in the evaluation of the teacher's programs. For example, by keeping annotated files of students' work teachers are able to see what progress is being made and how successful their programs are.

In addition to those already mentioned you need to keep program records to ensure that all aspects of mathematics are covered. You will need to keep notes on the areas covered in:
- introductory sessions;
- workshops; and
- other mathematical experiences (these can be detailed in your work program or on a separate sheet.

Departmental or ministerial guidelines and school policy and program documents can provide a basis for a content checklist. Supplement this with a checklist of problem-solving strategies and co-operative group skills (see pages 96 and 97 for examples). Each week highlight focus points covered. This acts as an ongoing record and as a reminder of areas that still need to be covered.

Some teachers assess the balance of their program at the end of each week, month, unit or term and then address any issues that have been overlooked. Some areas may only need to be covered in small group activities while others may be more suited to whole class activities, perhaps during introductory sessions. Remember that it is the teacher who is in the best position to make decisions about the needs of his/her students.

7

INTRODUCTORY AND WORKSHOP ACTIVITY IDEAS

Although this Project Maths approach emphasises real life, independent student investigations the teacher must also model and teach skills, concepts and strategies.

Resources for ideas are often limited and sometimes difficult to locate quickly. In this chapter we provide some ideas that we know work, and that will assist teachers in providing a balanced program. These activities have been primarily designed as introductory and workshop activities. The areas covered are:

- Counting
- Pattern and order
- Place value
- Fractions and decimals
- Area
- Perimeter
- Time
- Volume
- Spatial relations/geometry
- Visual representation/statistics
- Length
- Money
- Mass
- Computation

While we have listed these areas individually, in practice they are interrelated and best taught in meaningful contexts. Teachers should choose activities from those listed to teach and model specific skills as the need arises.

Don't forget to allow time to reflect on and verbalise strategies used during activities. For example, did students count on? How did they work out what double was?

Figure 7.1 Guide to the format used in this chapter

Mathematical content covered	Teacher's Notes, Activities, Ideas
Roughly in developmental order Mathematical skills and concepts have been indicated to assist with planning Examples of problem-solving activities have been included at the end of each section (ideally these would be related to your integrated studies)	Many ideas can be applied and reapplied to many levels (e.g. the Place value game 'Mastermind' can be made more difficult by increasing the number of digits used Teachers should select and adapt ideas according to the needs of their students and classroom focus.

A NOTE ABOUT CALCULATORS AND COMPUTATION

As we promote the development of skills within real life problems some numbers may be large or involve decimals. This is where the use of a calculator is beneficial. The calculator is useless without some knowledge of 'reasonableness' of results. You will need to encourage students to estimate before using the calculator and practise the skills of rounding off, recognising basic number facts and using problem-solving strategies such as identifying and choosing the correct operation.

An introductory or workshop session on calculator skills, for example using the memory, may be applicable. See also p. 18.

Counting

Prenumber   These activities could be done with a variety of concrete materials; for example: counters, toys, leaves etc.

Sorting objects:
- Students order in any way they like (tell your friend or class why you chose that way).
- Specific sorting (teacher directed): e.g. put all the blue toys in a group.
- Teacher groups objects and asks the students why they think this was done.
- Ask students to add objects to sort into groups or add objects to groups.

Ordering
- Read *Don't Forget The Bacon* by Pat Hutchins. On separate strips of paper write: *six farm eggs*; *a cake for tea*; *a pound of pears*; and *don't forget the bacon*. Ask students to order them. Make this more difficult by covering some words.
- Cut out two sets of the same shapes in various sizes. These could be stuck onto the whiteboard. Ask students to find the matching shapes and order in some way: e.g. by size, in a pattern etc.
- Put objects or students in order from tallest to smallest. Ask why they have been placed in that order. Ask for volunteers to add other students to the line in the correct positions.
- Put stones, rice, macaroni and sand into film containers. Have students put them into order: e.g. by the sound made when shaken.
- Have students order shades of color from a paint color chart.

Pattern
- Ask students to match, continue or make their own patterns. Use a variety of materials (see Sorting above).
- Ask one student to sit with his/her back to you. Play two notes on a xylophone. Ask the student find the same notes (without looking).
- Ask students to bring old neckties to school. Sort and classify these according to their patterns.
- Go outside and find patterns in the environment.
- Using attribute blocks, start a pattern. Ask students to finish this pattern. With experience vary the difficulty. Include more than one attribute: e.g. Big, small, big etc. Big red, small red, big blue, etc.
- Ask students to cut out pictures from magazines to make a pattern: e.g. flowers, animals. (Ideally, this would fit into the classroom theme.)

One-to-one correspondence

One-to-one correspondence can be reinforced informally. For example:
- In the dress-up corner ask students to put on one piece of clothing each.
- Appoint monitors to give out one pair of scissors each, etc.
- Give out a pile of counters and a pile of another group of objects e.g. farm animals. Ask questions. Are there more farm animals than counters? Encourage students to find a variety of ways to check this.

Learning number names
- Play Snap, but say the 'number' matched instead of saying 'snap'.
- Act out number rhymes and play counting games. Improvise on these, e.g.:
  One, two, I love you.
  Three, four I want more.

Recognise numbers: cardinal

- Draw number cards then cut them in half. Students must rejoin them and say the numbers.
- Play dice games: e.g. two players roll a dice and step out the number rolled. The first to 10, 20, or the end of the room wins.
- Play flashcard games.
- Draw a number in the air. Students must say or write down the number, or in pairs have one student draw the number on the other's back with their finger. Each partner gets two guesses to say the correct number, then they swap over.

Recognise numbers: ordinal

- Have a race outside. Hand out 1st, 2nd and 3rd cards before the race. Students put these in order on a ledge as their turn comes up.
- Teach the song 'The Twelfth Day of Christmas'.
- Read the story of the 'Billy Goats Gruff'. Students play the roles of the 1st, 2nd and 3rd goats.
- Read the *Chicken Book* by Garth Williams. Do a substitution and/or cloze exercise in place of the ordinal numbers and events.

Number words

- Play Bingo. Show the number word; students make a match if they have the numeral on their board (or vice versa). See also Pattern & Order (ordering numerals and words on p. 40).
- Hold up cards with number words written on them. Students must get into groups of that size: e.g.

- Play Snap using number words instead of letters.
- Place number words on large cards and attach to students. Without speaking they must put themselves in order.

Count by ones

- Teach the poem 'When I Was One' by A. A. Milne (from *Now We Are Six*).

Count by ones, twos, etc.

- Make counting patterns on strips of cards. Ask students to fill them in and/or work out what they are counting by. Some students could make their own cards for others.

> 1, —, —, 4, —, 6, —, —, —

- Draw a large number line on the cement with chalk or put masking tape on the carpet. Two players stand either side. Ask them to jump or step by 1's (or 2's etc.).
- This last can be adapted by using a dice or starting at different points along the line and aiming to get to a 'magic number'.

Different starting/ stopping points

- Find small objects to fit into larger objects: e.g. milk cartons into a box, infant squares onto a large piece of paper, Unifix into a milk carton etc. Guess and then check the number that fit. You could vary this by making it a race or by asking students to do the activity in groups. Each player only puts in a specified number: e.g. 10, then it's the next person's turn.
- Draw circles on a page, marking evenly by 1's from 0–9.

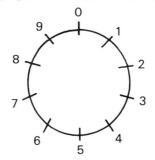

By using a ruler to join the last digit of any counting pattern, you come up with a repetitive design.

Fours ④ , ⑧ , 1 ② , 1 ⑥ , 2 ⓪ , 2 ④ , 2 ⑧

Students can compare patterns.

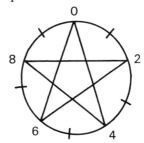

- Make a class or individual board game.
- Place number cards on a blackboard ledge. Students close eyes while you remove one or two cards. They must guess which ones are missing.

Counting by large numbers

- Play the game 'Buzz' but make the specified number large: e.g. count by 100's and buzz at 1000.
- Have students make and use their own rulers.
- Use a calculator to work out patterns with large numbers: e.g. 125, 165, 205 . . .

Forwards/backwards

- Teach the song 'Ten Green Bottles Hanging on the Wall'.

Problem solving

- How many rice bubbles would there be in a pack?
- By using a road map or atlas, work out how far it is between different suburbs, cities, countries.
- How many coins do you need to make a money trail from one end of the breezeway to the other?

Pattern and order

Match a pattern
- Clap out a rhythm and have students copy.
- Play What's In My Club?
  The teacher writes a list of numbers, letters, words or shapes on the board and students guess what other numbers would be in the club: e.g.

What's in my club?	
Yes	No
25	13
64	10
4	6
9	20

Answer: all square numbers.
- Combine several attributes e.g. colour, size and shape, to make a pattern for the rest of the class or for a partner to continue.
- Have students complete matrix patterns. With experience they can make up their own problems for others to solve.

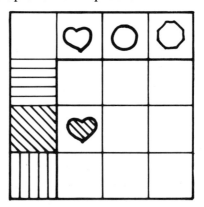

Continue a pattern
- Draw shapes, numbers, letters etc. on the board. Ask for a volunteer to add the next part of the patterns: e.g. 3, 7, 16, 35 (double plus 1, then double plus 2, double plus 3).

Doubling/halving
- Use a calculator to double and halve large numbers. Ask students to record the patterns they find.
- Read *All Fall Down* by Brian Wildsmith. Ask students to describe the pattern of size when the animals are balancing.

Recognise a pattern
- Read a story or teach a song with a repetitive, predictable story-line: e.g. 'There was an old woman who swallowed a fly'. Ask students to guess what will happen next. As an alternative or extension, do a substitution with the repetitive pattern.
- Draw up a 12×12 number grid on a large piece of paper. Ask students to come out and circle a counting pattern. This exercise can also be given to individuals or small groups of students.

Make a pattern
- Make some pattern strips, e.g.:

> # 172, 173, 175, 178, ___, ___

Ask students to guess what comes next.
- Ask students to write some of their own pattern strips to swap with others. This can be adapted by leaving gaps for students to fill in, e.g.:

> # 7.21, 7.23, ___, ___, ___, 7.27

Decimals
- Use grids or dot arrays to make patterns.

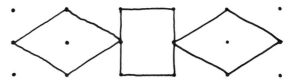

- Display a large blank grid (on the blackboard or overhead projector) and ask a student/s to come out to the front of the class to plot co-ordinates you give: e.g. 'Draw a line from A6–B7'. Students could create their own grid instructions for others to complete.

Ordering
- Read the story 'The 3 Billy Goats Gruff'. Dramatise the story or manipulate the characters using a flannelboard.

Numbers and words
- Ask volunteers to line up in front of the class. Give each a number card to hold in front of themselves. Ask them to unjumble to line up from: largest to smallest, smallest to largest, or in another pattern, e.g.:

Before/after

- Ask students to close their eyes while you mix up the line (above): either time them reordering or ask another student to fix up the line.

Greater than/less than

- Play quick quiz games orally with teams or as a written exercise.
- Draw up a number line or time line and ask students to put in the correct dates. This can be done on paper or use flashcards and masking paper to do it with a group.
- Play the game 'Higher or Lower'. The teacher or nominated student thinks of a number: e.g. between 0–50 or 1000–2000 and then responds to guesses by saying 'higher' or 'lower'.
  Adaptations:
  1. Allow only five or ten guesses. In this way teams can play each other or the teacher can challenge the students.
  2. Put numbers on cards hidden inside envelopes and call the game 'The Newest Price is Right'.
- Use sports results to order individual team member's achievements: e.g. the player who shot the most basketball goals.

Problem solving

- What is the largest/smallest number you can make with the numerals 0–9? The teacher chooses numbers at random. Each player must record the digit on their prepared number strip before the next number is chosen.
  See Place Value for an adaption of this idea using addition and subtraction.

Place value

Place value is a difficult concept to teach within an integrated program. Include Place value often in introductory activities. There are also many suitable calculator activities that can be used to reinforce Place value during activity time or in workshops.

Make models of numbers

- Show a card or write a number on the board for students to represent on:
  - an abacus
  - with Montessori cards
  - MAB equipment
  - in another way
  (This can be a teacher or student led activity done in pairs or in small groups.)
- To extend this activity ask students for statements about what they have done, for example: *First I put 342 on the abacus; to make 642 I just had to add 300.* The same or an adapted version of this activity can be used to represent numbers involving tenths.

- Use an abacus or MAB equipment to show a number. Ask students to represent this in the numerical form with pen and paper.

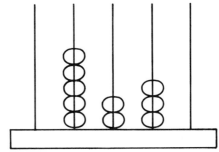

Renaming units
Extended notation

- Using MAB equipment, ask students to show you how to exchange units and longs after they get more than ten. Ask them to verbalise and/or record the reasons for doing this e.g.:

  135 = 1 flat + 2 longs + 15 units

  or 135 = 1 flat + 3 longs +   5 units

  or 135 = 100 + 30 + 5.

- Play the game 'Make a flat' (use MAB materials).

  Up to four players take turns to roll a dice. They are given the number of units by a 'banker' according to the number rolled. When they reach ten units they can request to exchange them for longs. The winner is the first to acquire ten longs (which can be exchanged for a flat).

- Play the game 'Break a flat'.

  This is a backwards version of 'Make a flat' (above). Players start with a flat and must roll the dice, forfeiting units and longs until they have nothing left. The first to lose all their units is the winner.

Calculators

- Tell students that the 5 and 7 keys are broken and ask them to work in groups to solve the problem of finding the answer to the question: 578 + 725 (use less digits with infant students). Students will naturally start using extended notation. Encourage them to use a variety of operations. Make a class list of ways to solve the problem. (This activity can be repeated using different numbers.)

- Enter a number: e.g. 347. Ask students to make 307, then have them explain how they did it.

Ordering numbers

- Find a number in the phone book that adds up to forty. Discuss the digits that will be needed. For example, if there are many 0's in the phone number, the other digits will have to be large.

- Ask for four or more volunteers to stand in a row in front of the class. Give each a number using two or three digits repeated: e.g. 5051, 1151, 5015, 5115. Ask them to order themselves. This may seem easy to observers, but it is not so easy for the volunteers, so it causes great audience participation.

- Ask students to make cards using only two or three different digits in a four digit number (for infants use smaller combinations in two or three digit numbers). Use these for a whole grade or in a small group activity.
- Play the game 'Place Value Bingo'.
  1 Students draw a 2 × 3 grid:

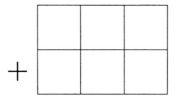

$=$ answer

  2 Shuffle number cards (0–9) then show one at a time. Students place these numbers anywhere in the grid to either make the largest or smallest number when both are added (numbers must be placed before the next is shown). If the largest number is required the largest numbers should be written in the hundreds column. Unfortunately you never know which number will come next, and taking a gamble adds to the excitement.

  Alternatively the bottom number can be subtracted.

Problem solving

- Draw an odometer on the whiteboard. Use Blu Tack and number cards to show a distance travelled. Ask questions: e.g. 'How many kilometres do I need to travel to make the odometer show 17 000 km?' or 'What is the next palindromic number?'

| 1 | 6 | 7 | 8 | 9 |

- Play the game 'Mastermind'.
  The teacher selects a number, e.g. 456, but does not tell the class. Students guesses are recorded on a chart with the number of correct digits and how many are in the correct position shown. Students continue to guess until they reach the correct number.

number guessed	correct digits	correct place
400	1	1
300	0	0
406	2	2
460	2	1
416	2	2
426	2	2
456	3	3

Calculators
- Create patterns on the calculator: e.g.
$$9 \times 2 = 18$$
$$99 \times 2 = 198$$
$$999 \times 2 = 1998$$
Ask students to guess what would come next.

Fractions and decimals

Informal use of ½ and ¼
- Make sandwiches — cut in ½'s, then in ¼'s.
- Cut fruit into pieces — would you rather have ¼ or ½?
- Put a piece of rope along the floor. Ask students to walk ½ way, then ¼ way etc.

Make ½ and ¼
Outdoor games
- Run, hop ½ way, ¼ way etc.
- Fold paper in ½, ¼. How many shapes are there?
- Give students a piece of string or a stick. Get them to find objects ¼ or ½ the size.

Record/name ½ or ¼
- Cut different shapes into two or four pieces. Jumble them and give a piece to all students. Ask them to make their shape whole. This can be done in silence.
- Extend this by asking students to make written statements about what they have done.
- Use a fraction cake to introduce other fractions.
- Give students a fraction card and ask students to work out how many pieces their cake is divided into.

$$\boxed{\frac{1}{8}}$$

- Paper Folding. Pose the challenge: 'What is the most amount of times any piece of paper can be folded?'
A further challenge: 'Before opening your folded paper work out how many divisions it will be folded into.'

Count by fractions
- Play 'Buzz' using ¹⁄₁₀ or mix with decimals, e.g. ¹⁄₁₀, .2, ³⁄₁₀, .4.
- Ask students to cut square paper into two triangles. Lay them on

the floor and count by ½'s.
- Take your pulse in 30 seconds, 15 seconds or 5 seconds. Multiply by two, four or twelve to work out your pulse rate per minute. Try this after sitting, walking and running.

- Place masking tape on the floor, or draw chalk on the ground outside, in the shape of a large square: e.g. 2 × 2 metres. Ask a volunteer to walk ¼ or ½ way around from a corner, then another to walk a ¼ around from another point (not a corner, etc.).
- To make this harder, draw a large triangle and ask them to do the same. The distance walked can vary. As an alternative give instructions using decimals.

Find fractional parts of groups

- Give students a pile of counters and ask them to find a fraction: e.g. ⅙ of 12. Ask 'How many do you have?'.
- Use a newspaper page to work out the fraction devoted to advertising.
- Ask students to form into groups. Of a group of four ask ¼ to leave (etc.).

Compare fractions

- Read *Dad's Diet* by Barbara Comber.
- Use the fraction cake to compare fractions: e.g. ⅓ and 2/6 of a cake.
- Fill clear jars ¼, ½, ¾ full of water. Ask students to put them in order and make a statement about the jars.
- Divide packets of Smarties and pose questions: e.g. 'Would you rather have 3/10's or ¼?'.

Decimals

- When introducing decimals use materials that can be divided into tenths.

Calculators

- Ask students to use a calculator to find out about .1. They will probably add until finding that 10 × .1 = 1. Ask co-operative groups to record all their findings on butcher's paper. Share the groups' work.
- Play the 'Decimal Make or Break a Flat' games (on p. 43), rename Make or Break units as .1.

Decimal fractions

- Ask co-operative groups to make a fraction or decimal number line on a metre strip, e.g.:

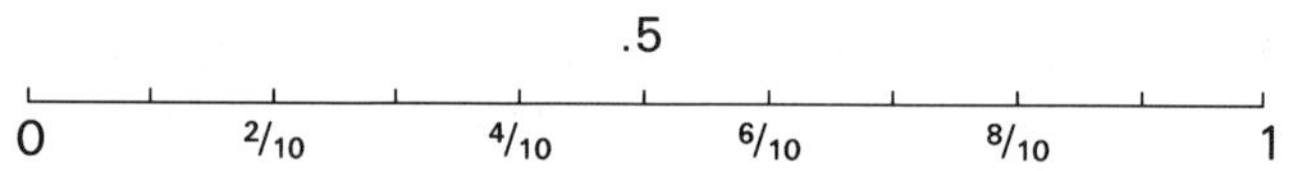

- Draw a large wall and have smaller copies for small groups. Ask students to write on the bricks the decimal and fraction.

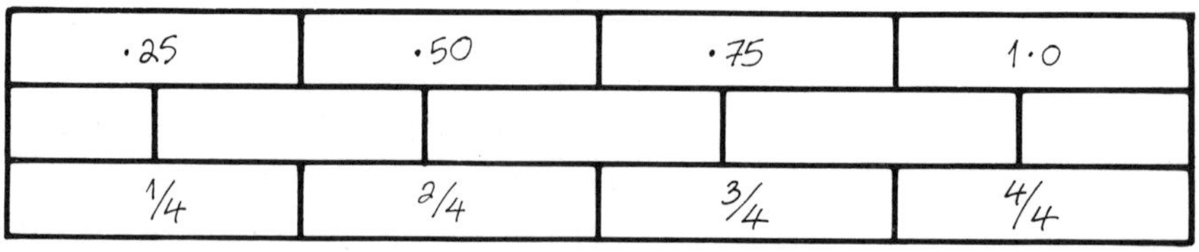

- Play a quick quiz game: 'Is ⅓ larger or smaller than .20?' (etc.).

0   .20   ½   ¾   1.0

- Use another number line and frame with vulgar fractions. Ask students to tell you the decimal equivalent.
- Ask students to calculate the mass in grams of ½ a packet of pasta, flour, etc. Ask them to write the findings as decimal fractions.

- If a ball was dropped from a height of sixty-four metres and bounced ½ its height each time, how high was the ninth bounce? 64, 32, 16, 8, 4, 2, 1, ½, ¼, ⅛.
- Plan a garden plot. Give clues: e.g. You will need a ¼ more space for pumpkin than carrots. _____ needs to grow at the front for the sun, etc.
- Plan a party menu. Make a list of guests and then calculate the food needed.

Area

Awareness ⟨
a⟩

groups —
Fractions

- Cut two matching shapes out of a sheet of paper and place this on ⟨ov⟩erhead projector. Shine these two shapes onto the black⟨... stu⟩dents in two teams and let the first member of ⟨... wh⟩o can be first to colour in the entire area ⟨... w⟩inner gets one point for their team. ⟨... st⟩udents have had a turn.

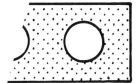

⟨...⟩ the floor with chalk. Ask students to pre-⟨...⟩s it will take lying down to cover the whole ⟨... fra⟩ctions then try it with larger and smaller

⟨... as⟩k how many paintings will cover the pin

- Plac⟨e ... wh⟩ite paper on an easel. Ask students whether they think ⟨they c⟩ould cover the whole area of the paper in one minute. Then give them a small brush. Have four or five students paint at once.

Comparison of regular and irregular shapes
- Cut out shapes in cellophane. Ask students to guess which has the largest area. Check by holding the shapes against each other on the overhead projector.

- Give students a photocopied sheet (see page 98) of pairs of shapes. Students predict which of each pair has the largest area, they can then cut out each shape and test their predictions by overlapping them.

Comparison by covering

- Cut out a number of regular and irregular shapes then show them to pairs of students. Ask them to predict which will have the largest area. The partners can then test their prediction by covering each shape with objects such as counters, Unifix cubes, buttons etc.
- Read the story of 'The Princess and the Pea' by Hans Christian Andersen. Discuss the story and then show the class a blanket and a quilt. Explain that these were the actual covers that the Princess used (imagination is good for the soul!). Ask the class to predict which has the largest area. In two groups have the students test their predictions by covering them with a variety of objects. (It might be valuable to discuss what would be the most appropriate sized objects to measure with, such as books, small blackboards etc. rather than small counters.)

Using a common unit

- Draw two shapes on a transparency on the overhead projector. Students predict which will have the largest area. Two students can test the predictions by placing a variety of objects on the shapes and counting them. Give one student only large shapes such as lids etc. and the other only small shapes. With approximately the same area the answers will be very different. Students should be able to describe the reasons for this difference. Now repeat this activity using a common unit such as Unifix cubes.
- Measure the area of a variety of transparent shapes on the overhead projector with Unifix cubes. (Remember, students predict first then test their predictions.)
- Cut out a large number of 5 cm felt squares. One student uses a piece of wool to make the outline of a shape on the flannelboard. The class predicts how many felt squares it will take to cover the outlined area. One student can then test this by covering the shape with the squares. Repeat this with different shapes outlined in wool.
  This can be extended by changing the shape or size of the squares.

Formal length × width

- Using the flannelboard and felt squares or the overhead projector and Unifix cubes make a rectangle four × five units in perimeter. Ask for a volunteer to cover the area with the felt squares or cubes. Have the grade calculate the area of the shape by adding the squares or cubes. Ask some volunteers to explain how they came to their answer. Select a variety of answers until one student suggests the 'Area = length × width' concept. If necessary demonstrate with four rows of five counters, ask the students to count the rows by fives — 5, 10, 15, 20 — refer to the multiplication equation $4 \times 5 = 20$, then describe the length $\times$ width theory.

Now allow students to practise with their shapes or cubes on the flannelboard or overhead projector.

- Use Geoboards to make rectangular or square shapes. Students count the nails and multiply length $\times$ width to calculate the area. This could be done as a class activity or in pairs with students making shapes for their partner to calculate.

Comparison using grids

- After the activities above students will realise the difficulty of using counters and other materials to measure with (slipping etc.). Using the overhead projector and a shape transparency overlay a transparent grid sheet (with squares the same size as the Unifix cubes). Students can count these squares to calculate and compare areas etc.
- Have students place objects from around the room on the grid transparency and calculate their surface areas.
- Place a large sheet of grid paper on the board and ask one volunteer to draw any picture on it. The student must follow the rule that all lines in the picture must follow the grid lines. Ask students to estimate the area of the picture. The class can now count the grid squares to check their estimations.
- Place a transparent grid of sixteen squares on the overhead projector and tell students to imagine this is a bar of chocolate. Four people want to share it but they must each get a piece with the same area. How many different ways can it be shared out equally? Get students to estimate first, brainstorm and then test their suggestions.

Introduction of formal units

- Using the grid transparency on the overhead projector, place a transparent colored shape on the grid. Ask students to calculate its area. For example it might have an area of eight units. Explain to the class that each grid square is actually one centimetre square, ask them to calculate the area of the shape in centimetres. Try this with a number of other regular shapes and then some objects from around the room.

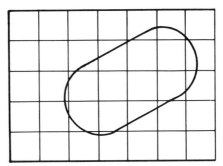

- You can make this even more challenging by changing the value of the grid squares. For example, have the class imagine each grid square is 2 cm square or 5 cm or any number that the class can multiply.
- Have the class brainstorm a list of suggestions for working out the area of the blackboard, school carpark, netball court etc. This problem could be tackled by the whole class or small groups. The need for a larger unit (metre) will become obvious.

Area/perimeter relationships

- Place a pile of cm cubes in the centre of the floor. Ask students to work in pairs and collect twenty cubes. They can then make any rectangle or square shape using these cubes. Ask them to calculate the surface area and place their information on a large class chart. Ask:
  - 'Are all surface areas the same?'
  - 'Why?'
  This activity could be extended by giving out more or less cubes and comparing the results.

Volume/surface area relationships

- Ask students to collect one box each and calculate its surface area and perimeter. Then compare this with other students. Can they find any pattern?
- Use plasticine to make a cube and calculate its surface area. What happens to the surface area when you cut the cube in half?
- Make a die and compare the surface area when made and unmade.

Informal investigations of circles

- Show a circle made from an overhead projector transparency and ask students to suggest how they could measure its area. Let them measure with a variety of objects on the overhead projector.
- Rule a cm-square grid on a transparency and place a variety of different-size coloured transparent circles on the grid. Have the class estimate then count the number of squares.
- Brainstorm and list other ways to work out the area of a circle: e.g. cutting out and re-organising the pieces etc.
- Display four circles the same size and ask small groups to work out the area of the four circles combined.
- Empty a money box onto the floor. 'How can we work out the area covered and the area not covered?' This problem could be posed for small co-operative groups to work out.

Border areas

- Use the overhead projector, place 5 cm squares of paper on it and explain that you are making a path. Have the class calculate the area as you go.
  Now tell the students that you are going to make a patio that is 4×3 pavers. Ask them what its area will be. (300 cm²)

25 cm²   50 cm²   100 cm²

- Take two pavers out to make a pond. What is the area now?

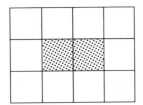

$$300\text{cm}^2$$
$$-\quad 50\text{cm}^2$$
$$=\ 250\text{cm}^2$$

Problem solving
- Read *The Quilt* by Ann Jonas and work out the cost of making a patchwork quilt. (Why not make one too? This could be a group or individual effort.)
- Play 'The Quilt Game' (see pages 99 and 100).
- Calculate the cost of:
  - painting the classroom walls
  - carpeting the classroom at $100 per square metre
- Conservation of area.
  Trace around a large object such as a car. Remove the object (only if you have a licence!) and cover the area with newspaper. How many sheets did this take? Rearrange the sheets; do they cover the same area?

Perimeter

Awareness of edges and boundaries
- Outdoor activity: during physical education sessions define the playing space by having students play 'follow the leader' around the perimeter of a netball/basketball court. Make sure you use the term 'perimeter'.
- Draw shapes on the floor with chalk. Have students estimate how many students it will take standing, sitting or lying to cover the whole perimeter of the shape. Test out the estimations and then try an even larger shape.
- Use a set of farm animals and have students build perimeter fences for them (extend this by allowing them to make farm buildings, machinery etc.).
- Play the 'Perimeter Game' (see page 101). Two people can play game. One starts by placing three counters on the square shapes and the other puts his/her counters on the circles. Take it in turns to throw a dice and move counters around the perimeter of the board. The first person to get around the perimeter and place their counters on the opponent's shape wins the game.

Awareness of perimeter
- Have students use Geoboards to create their own shapes. 'Do shapes need edges?' 'What are these called?'
  Have volunteers try to change the shape but keep the same perimeter length, e.g. twenty nails.
- Make a circle from a piece of rope approximately 5 m long. Select six students at a time to stand inside the rope and change its perimeter shape.

- Play the 'Perimeter Dance'. Draw a large shape on the floor (chalk will dust off). Play some music and let the class dance around inside the shape. When the music stops they must stand on the perimeter. The last student to do so is out. Keep going until you have a winner.
- To make it harder (and more fun) try alternating actions: for example, the first time the music stops the students must stand on the perimeter and the second time they must sit. The last student is still out and so is anyone who stands or sits at the wrong time.

Informal comparisons

- Make two groups of four students. Give each group a circle of rope, one circle slightly larger than the other. Have each group make the perimeter of a shape by standing inside the rope. Have the rest of the class identify the shapes and then ask which they think has the largest perimeter. Ask 'How can you check this?' Then test their theories out.

Formal units

- On the overhead projector use Unifix cubes to make a square. Ask the students to tell you what the perimeter is equal to. Explain that every cube is 1 cm long, how many centimetres long do they think the perimeter is? Try this with a variety of different sized shapes.
- On a large sheet of paper draw a 5 cm grid. Draw a rectangle on this grid. Now ask the students to calculate the perimeter length. Ask for volunteers to try to draw a different shape with the same perimeter.
- Hold up two large paper shapes, for example a rectangle and a triangle. Ask students to estimate which has the biggest perimeter. Let volunteers measure this in centimetres.
- Have ten students make a circle. Students estimate how many metres the perimeter would be. A volunteer could then use a trundle wheel to check the answer.

Area/perimeter relationships

- Draw some squares on the blackboard in the following patterns:

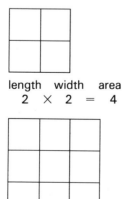

length width area
2   ×   2   =   4

3   ×   3   =   9

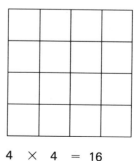

4   ×   4   =   16

- Ask students to predict the next square to be drawn or ask a volunteer to come to the blackboard and do it.
- Ask if students can see any patterns.
- Ask questions like 'If the length and width was 100 cubes, what would the area be?'
- Using five, six or seven counters make a number of shapes (these can be recorded on graph paper). What is the perimeter for each? Can students find any patterns?
- Have students use Geoboards to make different shapes with the same perimeters and record their findings.

Diameter and circumference
- Ask students to bring a collection of round objects to school. Ask them to measure the diameter and circumference, recording their findings. What do they find?

Diameter	Circumference
1. 2. 3.	

- Ask the class to find the circumference of the school oval but have them estimate first.

Perimeter in the environment
- Have the class brainstorm as many places as possible where perimeter fencing is used, then classify the list:
  e.g. • safety
       • aesthetics
       • property etc.
- Place three leaves on the overhead projector. How can we determine the perimeter? Let students make suggestions and then test them out. Try this with a variety of other objects.

Problem solving
- Try the matchstick puzzles on the overhead projector.
- How many milk cartons will we need to make
  • a wall?
  • a castle? (you will need to designate the dimensions)
- In pairs, use twenty-four sticks to make a square. Take turns to take away one, two or three sticks. Whoever takes away the last stick is the winner. Can students work out how to win every game?
- How much wire would be needed to make a three-strand fence around the school ground?
- What is the circumference of a circle? How many rotations would be needed for the circle to travel 1 km?
- Measure the perimeter of a person.

Time

....

Sequencing
- Jumble and unjumble picture cards made from a book or class topic such as the growth stages of a plant.
- Getting dressed: have ready a number of articles of clothing from the dress-up box. Ask students to put them on and off in the correct sequence. You could make a relay race out of this activity.
- Read *Who Sank the Boat?* by Pamela Allen and draw or trace the pictures of the animals in the story. Attach these drawings to pieces of felt for the flannelgraph board or to sticks to use as stick puppets. Then have students retell the sequence of events from the story.
- In small groups have students arrange themselves in order of their date of birth.
- Read *Anna's Day* by Peggy Blakely and discuss the sequence of activities during the day. Students can compare this with their own day. Then each student can select a time and draw what they would be doing at that time. Combine these and make a class poster.

Awareness of time cycles/routines of the day
- Make a class poster showing what the class was doing every hour for each day of the week. Students could then try an individual one for their own project.
- Give each child a small square of paper and ask them to draw something they do at school. Have a large paper chart on the board:

before school	before play	at play	before lunch	at lunch	before afternoon play	at afternoon play	at play	before home time	at home

Each student can glue their picture into the correct place and you can discuss events that occur at specific times.
- Draw clock faces to show important times of the day at home and school. Display them under your class clock so children can match the times as they occur.
- Plant a broad bean seed in a jar. Observe what happens each day and record this information on a class chart.

- Read *The Very Hungry Caterpillar* by Eric Carle. Discuss the events in the book then record the cycle of changes the caterpillar went through.

The hour as shown on the clock face
- Play 'Lotto' with time. Give pairs of students a photocopied time sheet with the twelve hours visible (see page 102). Students select any six times and circle them. Pull out any six time-cards from a hat and the pair with the most time matches wins. (You could also use these cards to play Bingo.)
- Make twelve cards with clock faces to hang around students' necks. Ask for twelve volunteers. Place the cards on students' backs so they cannot see their own time but others can. The group must then get themselves into order from 1 o'clock to 12 o'clock without speaking. This is a great co-operative group activity. Repeat until all students have had a turn.

The hour as shown on the clock face
- Play 'What's the time Mr Wolf?'.
- Play 'Time Race'. Divide the class into two rows standing parallel. Show the clock face at any o'clock time and the first pair races to tell the correct time; then the second pair, and so on. Each winner gets a point for their team.
- Make a large set of 'Time Dominoes' and play this with the class:

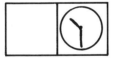 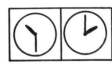 

Experience with measured periods of time
- Play some music for a set period of time (say twenty seconds). Let students listen first and then estimate how many times they can complete a given activity in that period of time: e.g. hop, tie and untie their shoe-laces, take off and on their jumper etc. Have students record their estimations then test them as you play the music again.

Experience with measured periods of time
- Have students try to smile for one minute without stopping.
- Have students close their eyes and guess specific time intervals — thirty seconds, one minute, two minutes etc. Have them keep their eyes shut and put up their hand when they think the time is up.
- Have students predict then check how many times they can do a variety of tasks in a minute. For example: clap, stamp their feet,

blink etc. Ask what would happen to the answers if they doubled or halved the time span.
- Outdoor activity: How far can students run, skip, step etc. in one minute? Once again, guess then check.
- Ask students to estimate how far they could run, hop, skip, or even crawl or roll, in a given period of time. Students write down their estimations, test them and then record their results for comparison with their estimations.

Days of the week
- Keep an individual or class diary. It could focus on the weather, daily events, feelings etc.
- Read *The Very Hungry Caterpillar* by Eric Carle. Divide a long sheet of paper into the days of the week. Place students into seven groups to discuss what event should go into each section and then draw this and place it onto the strip.
- Play 'Buzz' using the days of the week. Change the Buzz day regularly: e.g. Buzz on Sunday, then on Thursday, next Wednesday and then Saturday etc.

Time intervals of five and fifteen minutes
- Give students an understanding of a five minute period of time by having them lie down and listen to a piece of music for five minutes.

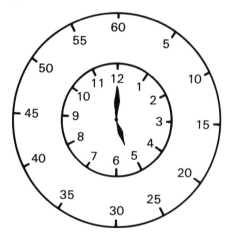

- Introduce the 'Five minute clock face' and ask students to tell you the time represented. This is a good oral activity and can be made into a variety of games such as Buzz, races etc.
- Write out a number of digital time cards, e.g. 10.20 6.55 .

  Ask for ten volunteers; place these students in two teams. Display the cards on the board ledge. One student from each team steps forward. Show one of the card times on the clock face and the two students race to point to the correct digital equivalent e.g. twenty past ten = 10.20.
- Add cards that include ½ past, ¼ past and ¼ to, etc. to the cards above and then try the game again.

Using operations
- Timetable exercises in either verbal or written form. For example: 'The Hurstbridge train was due at 1.15 but it arrived at 1.17. How late was it?'
- Have students calculate how many months, weeks and days old they are. (Make use of the calculator.)
- Have students take their pulse for ten or twenty seconds. They can then multiply their answers to calculate their pulse rate over one minute.

Problem solving
- If it takes one minute to make one cut through a log how long will it take to cut the log into 7 pieces? (Encourage students to draw their answers.)
- Ask students to make a device that will record an interval of time. (At Doreen Primary School Prep and Year 1/2 students made a minute hour-glass using two small cream bottles, and a water-clock from a yoghurt container.)
- Ask students if they can find out the origins of the names of the days and months or of the Chinese year names.
- Read *All in a Day* by Mitsumasa Anno and ask students to work out the time in different parts of the world. Why are they different?
- Have students analyse current road statistics. What is the safest or most dangerous time to travel?

Volume

Estimation
- Place a hoop on the floor and ask 'How many children do you think could stand in this hoop?' Students estimate, record these estimations and then test them out using volunteers. You could repeat this having the volunteers sit in the hoop and compare the results.
- Make an irregular shape on the floor with rope with the same perimeter as the hoop and try it again.
- Fill a small jar with jelly beans (or other small lollies). Students get two chances to estimate the total number: the first guess before counting begins and the second after counting ¼ or ½. Finish counting them together, with the closest estimate getting the lollies as a treat.
- Read *Phoebe and the Hot Water Bottle* by Terry Furchgott and Linda Dawson. Hold up a hot water bottle and a cup and ask students to estimate how many cups of water Phoebe would need to fill the hot water bottle. Estimate individually or in small groups, to discuss and agree on a number, then check. You could extend this by writing students' estimations on a poster in the shape of a hot water bottle. Students could write a statement about their estimation.

- Each day for a week read the class a book where the concept of 'volume' is referred to.

  For example:
  - *Teddy Bears Go Shopping*
    by Suzanna Gretz
  - *Mr Archimedes' Bath*
    by Pamela Allen
  - *Who Sank the Boat?*
    by Pamela Allen
  - *Dad's Diet*
    by Barbara Comber
  - *Something Absolutely Enormous*
    by Margaret Wild

  Put these books on display and ask students to tell you what was common or similar about them. Many elements of maths may be suggested. List them all on a chart but choose volume to focus your comparison on. You may also ask students to suggest examples of where volume or other concepts are found within the books.

Awareness of the capacity of containers

- Fill a milk carton with coloured water (tell the class it is 'magic water'). Then show the class four different capacity containers which are numbered from 1 to 4. Ask students to vote for the container they think will hold all of the 'magic water' from the milk carton.

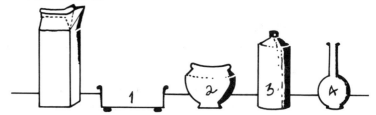

- Have four boxes of different capacity. Ask students to vote on the one that will hold the most blocks. Ask for volunteers to stack blocks into the boxes to check.

- Read the story of 'Goldilocks and the Three Bears'. Show a large bowl, a medium sized bowl and a small bowl. Ask students to estimate how many cups of oats each would hold. Check these estimations.

- Hold up a thimble or medicine glass. Ask students to estimate how many grains of rice would fit into it. Now check the estimations by filling it with rice then emptying the grains onto the overhead projector. The class can then count them together.

Direct comparison of two containers

- Ask for two volunteers to lend you one shoe each. Ask the class to estimate which shoe will hold the most rice. Have a volunteer fill one shoe with rice then empty it into the other shoe. Which held more? Ask for other volunteers and suggest filling shoes with other substances such as spaghetti or jelly beans.

- Fill a long thin container (spaghetti jar, Thermos or column jar etc.) with water. Provide a variety of different shaped containers and ask for a volunteer to find a container that holds the same amount of water. Check by pouring the water into the containers.
- Display two boxes, one already stacked with blocks and the other empty. Which holds more blocks? Ask a student to volunteer to stack the blocks from one box to the other. Don't count them, which held more?
- Display two boxes the same size but different shapes. Fill one with small objects such as Unifix cubes and the other with larger objects such as matchboxes. How do we find out which is the largest box?

NOTE: To help students keep count demonstrate the value of tallying, eg. ⊦⊦⊦ ||, whenever possible.

Capacity of containers using common units

- Have a large bowl of rice, a box and a number of different sized pouring containers (accessible somewhere in the room although not on display with the rice). Tell the class you have a problem. You have to fill the box with rice but you are not allowed to touch the bowl. How can you get the rice from the bowl into the box? Someone will probably suggest using a cup to transfer the rice. Get the pouring containers and ask for a volunteer to show you which one should be used. This should lead to a discussion about the use of the most appropriate-sized common unit. Ask students to guess how many cups it will take to fill the box. Now check it.
- Use the same cup to check how much rice it takes to fill a variety of objects. Once again, have students estimate first then get a volunteer to measure the rice with the cup. Use a scribe to keep a tally to check the estimations and so record the results for comparison.
- Show the class a container and ask them to estimate how many tablespoons of rice, or flour or even water would fit in it. Ask for a volunteer to measure and someone to keep a tally. Now tell the volunteer that the spoon must be held in the mouth (a little extra challenge)!
- Fill a box with MAB flats. Have students estimate how many are in the box. Now count them to find out. This can be done with smaller or larger objects as well.
- Give pairs of students a number of common objects such as twenty blocks or a handful of Unifix cubes. The pairs must then either find a container around the room that can be filled with their counters or you could have them make the appropriate sized container. Then have them report their findings back to the whole group.

Displacement as a measure of volume

- Read *Mr Archimedes' Bath* by Pamela Allen and ask the class to explain what happened.
- In small groups or as a class demonstration give students some plastic farm animals or Unifix cubes and a jar ¾ full of water. How many animals will need to be placed in the jar before the water overflows. Have students estimate first and then test their theory. Ask them to keep a record of their findings to present to the class.
- Refer back to the story and ask students to work in pairs and represent what happened (for example, using pictures, models, etc.). Present these to the class in share time.
- Have a variety of different sized zoo animals and a jar half full of water. Ask for suggestions as to which animals will displace the most water. Have volunteers test their predictions by placing their animal in the jar and marking a line where the water peaks with a texta.
- Write a class version using different characters (even class members or teachers) and a different location (such as the swimming pool) and publish it for your class library.

Choosing appropriate units of measurement

- Place two bowls of the same size on a table. Ask for two volunteers to take part in a race to fill the bowls with rice. When the students are ready, give one a teaspoon and the other a cup. This should lead to discussion about the need for an appropriate unit. (We call this 'Teacher's Revenge'!)
- Brainstorm to fill in a chart to suggest the most appropriate unit of measurement to compare containers, e.g.:

Containers to compare	Units to measure with
a cup and a glass	water, marbles, sand, flour
a bucket and a wheel barrow	rocks, dirt, water, sand
an egg cup and a medicine jar	rice, water, sugar

Formal units (litre)

- Have a litre milk container filled with water and a variety of other containers that are numbered. Ask students to note down which of the containers will hold the entire litre of water then test their predictions out.
- Make a class collection of litre containers such as milk cartons, soft drink bottles etc.

Volume related to height, base area and surface area

- In pairs ask students to make a box with twenty blocks. See how many other shapes they can make with the same number of blocks.
- Make some unusual shapes with blocks or Lego and see if pairs of students can copy them. Discuss how many cubes it took to make them.
- Make a number of boxes from cubes and have students work in small groups with one box to fill in a line of a class chart e.g.

names	height	length	width	total number of cubes
Salvatore Cathy	3	4	2	24
Sue Pat	6	5	6	180

- Discuss the findings.
- What sort of patterns can we find?

Fractional parts of a litre

- Display a clear 1 litre jar and cups. Ask students to estimate how many cups of macaroni it would take to fill the jar. Try it. Ask questions such as 'If it takes four cups to fill the jar and I put in only one cup what fraction have I put in?'
- Have a quick quiz: e.g. 'I bought a litre of milk for breakfast and my dad and I had one cup each. How much was left?'
- Ask students to write stories about fractionally filling or using parts of a litre.

Formal units to measure volume

- Cut out coloured transparent squares and put them on the overhead projector. Have students estimate how many cubes would fit onto each one. A volunteer can test these estimations. If the cubes are placed on the shapes on the overhead projector the class can easily count with the volunteer.
- How many centimetre cubes can fit into a matchbox. Have students estimate and then test their estimations.
- Try this with a number of other different size boxes.
- In small groups ask students to make a cube from centimetre cubes then use their information to fill in a class chart: 'What patterns can we find?'

Problem solving

- How many dishwashes can I get from a jar of washing up liquid?
- How many grains of rice in a packet?
- How many drops of water in a litre?
- Ask students to make a container that will hold exactly one litre of liquid. To make this harder ask them to design one that is environmentally friendly.

Spatial relations/geometry

Awareness of shape
- Make a 'feel it' bag and invite volunteers to come out to the front of the group to guess the contents by their shape. You could ask the volunteers to describe it first.
- Wrap objects and ask students to guess what they could be.
- Draw shapes on flashcards. Ask students to find things in the room that are that shape. You could also do this outside.
- Play 'Shape Bingo'.
- Try simple tangrams.

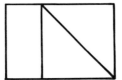 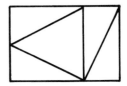

Recognition/naming shapes
- Make two of each of a number of different shapes. Sit students in a circle and pass one set out to the group. Ask students to lay them on the floor in front of them. Hide the other set in a box and ask a volunteer to pick a shape from the other set and keep it behind his/her back. Without looking at the shape, feel around the outside and guess who has its match. Allow students to walk around the circle before guessing.
- Make a set of velvet or sandpaper numbers or letters. Once again students place these behind their backs and try to guess what the shape is by feeling — not looking.
- Use a large Geoboard. Children take it in turns to make a shape that the others cannot see. They can describe it as they make it, the rest of the group guess what it is. The shape can be shown when guessed or after a specified number of guesses.
- Lay a trail of flashcards with shapes on them, on the floor. Roll a dice. The player walks that number and names the shape. Alternatively the player can be blindfolded and must be guided by an unblindfolded partner who describes the shape without naming it.
- Play a shape version of 'I Spy with My Little Eye', for example, 'I spy with my little eye a large, red, circle shape.' Let the other students guess the object.

Patterns with shape
- Using attribute blocks make a pattern, e.g.

What comes next? Have students explain how they know.
- Allow students to create their own patterns in pairs. To make this more difficult, make the shapes vary in thickness or size.

- Draw a shape, e.g.:

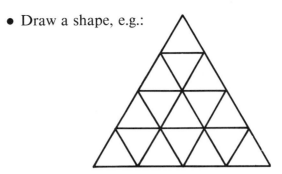

How many triangles are there? (Better look twice!) Now try it with a friend.

Left and right
- Try a shape matrix and have volunteers draw in the appropriate shape.

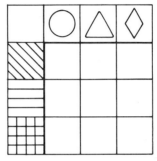

- Play 'Simon Says'. Give instructions such as 'Touch someone who is on your right with your left hand', etc.

Position in space
- Read the story *Where's Spot?* by Eric Hill. Play an outdoor game where students must stand next to, underneath or over partners and equipment.
- Read *Rosie's Walk* by Pat Hutchins. In pairs or small groups the class constructs an obstacle course in the classroom, e.g. Rosie walked over a table, under a chair, etc. Let the class draw their favourite part of the book; when finished place drawings in order to display around the room.

Rosie walks over the top of the hay stack with the fox on her tail

- Play 'Are you in my Club?' with symmetrical letters. Chart guesses on a large piece of paper. For example: 'A' is in the club. 'L' isn't. 'H' is, but 'Q' isn't.

Are you in my club?	
Yes	No
A	L
H	Q

Students are asked to elect letters that might be in the club. They must not state the rule until they are absolutely sure, if they guess incorrectly they lose.

Symmetry
- Make charts of numbers or the alphabet. Ask volunteers to come out and draw a line of symmetry on any symmetrical number or letter on the chart, e.g.:

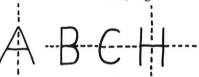

- Ask volunteers to draw or name shapes in nature that are symmetrical.
- Draw halves of various shapes and ask students to complete the other half.
- Cut out magazine pictures or faces. Cut them in half and ask students to draw the other side.

Relationship between 2D and 3D shapes
- Make a chain of paper dolls.
- Make a tangram and have volunteers make pictures by moving them on the overhead projector. Extension: students use tangram pictures to tell or illustrate a story.

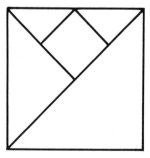

- Use the overhead projector to make shadows of hands, heads and other objects. Trace them onto a sheet of paper.
- Try this with attribute shapes at various angles.

Nets (outlines of 3D shapes)
- Ask students to make a fat or thin cylinder from a piece of paper. You could also specify the measurements.
- Show a diagram for a die or, as a challenge, ask students to make their own patterns for other shapes.
- Cut up food boxes, e.g. cereal boxes. Ask students to reconstruct. Have races and time students.

Angles
- Make some origami objects. Unfold the paper to find the angles.

Tessellations
- Ask students to make a list of where they might find tessellations in the environment (e.g. honeycombs, tiling etc.).
- Students can design some of their own with attribute blocks or rulers.

Shape and design
- How can a straight line be a curved line? Pose the question first then show a chart with the drawing of a right angle as shown in the example. Join matching numbers with a ruler. Students may be given time to draw some of their own.

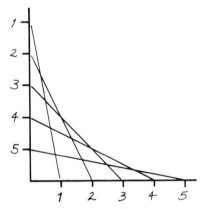

- Display a large Geoboard. Have children estimate how many squares could be made. Let children take it in turns to make squares using different coloured rubber bands. Tally the score as you go.

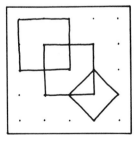

Point of view
- Play the computer game 'Ant Farm'.
- Place objects on a tray in the middle of a circle. Ask students to draw what they see. Jumble the drawings and decide where the artist was sitting.
- Draw the room or school from a bird's-eye view.

Points of the compass
Plans/grids

- Make a Treasure Hunt (inside or outside the class). Use clues like

| Walk 5 steps to the East for the next clue. |

- Get a copy of the school or a house plan. White out the names and ask students to label the rooms.
- Design a new playground.
- Play 'Battleships'.
- Use road-map grid references for students to find locations, chosen by yourself or the students.

Problem solving

- Give students a copy of a road-map page. What is the quickest route to . . . ?
- If a paddock is 200 metres × 100 metres, and is to be divided into 5 even sections, what size and shape could it be?

Visual representation/statistics

Representing two
objects to show
difference

- Read *Tiddalick the Frog who Caused a Flood* by Robert Roennfeldt. Ask students to draw Tiddalick before and after he drank the water. Have students write or dictate statements about the sizes of the frogs in their pictures.

- Place Unifix cubes in a number of piles on the floor. Ask students to think of their favourite colour. Now tell them you are going to count to fifty (or 100) and they have to make the biggest tower they can using only their favourite coloured cubes. Display these on a table and have the pairs or a small group make a record of what they have done and attach it to their towers.

- Put numbered slips of paper into a box (if you have thirty students you will need two lots of numbers 1 to 15). Students pick a piece of paper from the box and then find their partner, who has the same number. If you ask students to do this without talking this is a good co-operative activity. Have them stand back to back and determine who is biggest. This could be represented by drawing, writing or photography.
- Place counters in a row on the overhead projector so that the whole class can see easily and ask volunteers to make towers bigger or smaller than yours. Have the class discuss the relative sizes and difference between each tower.

One symbol representing one object using two-column representation

- Visually represent your class in a variety of ways. Thread coloured beads on strings, e.g. a red bead for girls and a green one for boys. Hang these around the room and ask for statements to explain which is longest etc.
- Give each student a small square of paper and ask them to draw something about themselves. Are they wearing shoes or runners? Did they have fruit for lunch or not? Then place them in two rows to compare.
- Have students take off one of their pieces of footwear. Put shoes in one row and sneakers in another. What is the most common footwear?
- Make a daily weather graph. For example:

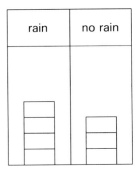

Just for fun appoint a weather forecaster.
- Ask students if they like peas. Have them stick a green circle onto a graph to represent their opinion.

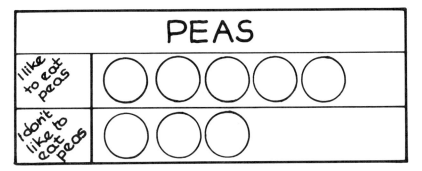

- Ask students to make a choice between two alternatives. If possible choose something topical or related to your class theme. For example, should the Olympics always be held in Athens? Should we have to wear a school uniform? Place this on a chart on a transparency on the overhead projector. Students place a counter in turn to represent their own view. Invite them to explain their decision. What does this information tell us?

One symbol representing one object using more than two columns

- Extend the ideas from the previous section by adding more variables e.g. 'What would you choose as your uniform colour?

One symbol representing more than one object

- Collect a large bank of information from the class, such as the eye colour of twelve family members. Display this information on a chart and ask for a volunteer to represent the information using beads threaded on string (make sure these strings are labelled but too short to hold all the beads). Discussion should lead to the teaching point of the need to represent more than one object with each bead. For example one bead represents ten eye colours.
- Extend this by collecting information that relates to your current theme and graph accordingly.

Use of grids

- Give each student a different size piece of paper to stick onto a class graph. During discussion students will realise that the paper representation of 'votes' need to be the same size. This is a good time to introduce a sheet made as a grid and have students shade in their particular square. Discuss why this is more accurate.
- Now try graphing a variety of issues that are relevant to your current area of study. You could consider graphing during your literature activities, e.g. what is the favourite book by a particular author?

Refinement to bar graphs

- Refer back to the earlier graphs and ask for suggestions to make these easier to read. Hopefully someone will suggest numbering the votes. Try this. Does it make reading the graph easier? Introduce the term 'bar graph'.
- In small groups give students a newspaper and ask them to cut out any bar graphs, for example weather maps, financial statements etc. In small groups ask them to prepare a report about their graph telling what they found out.
- Start a class graph collection.
- Send students in small groups to pace out set distances around the school then have them record this on a chart.
- Have a graph grid prepared but ask students for suggestions as to how we could represent large distances when, for example, we haven't got 310 spaces. This should lead to the suggestion of scale. Then try this using 1 cm to ten steps. Discuss the need for scale and refer back to the class newspaper graph collection.

Pictograms
- Use any current theme or the idea listed above to represent data using pictures.
  This could be done as a whole class consensus activity or ask small co-operative groups to represent the same/different information, then consider the appropriateness of the alternatives presented.

Locating position on a line — single axis
- Explain the concept of a time line and show one based on the school day:

9.00	10.30	12.00	2.15	3.30
come inside	play time	lunch time	play time	home time

- Give each student a timeline and have them mark in their own day for twenty-four hours (discuss the scale being used).
- Ask students to make a line map of the school corridor. Send a small group of volunteers to measure the corridor with a trundle wheel and mark in all the features:

- Make a strip map to show the distances between the school and the local shopping center or other known points in the area.
- Ask students a variety of questions, e.g.:
  - How far is it from x to y?
  - What is half way between x and y? etc.
  Don't forget the first number is always the horizontal axis, e.g. 7H.
- Show students how to enlarge or reduce a simple picture using a grid. This can be easily demonstrated on an overhead projector.
- Give students a maze to solve using grid references (see page 103). It could be photocopied onto an overhead projector transparency and volunteers could suggest the correct references and order.
- Give students street directories or atlases. Do a quick quiz where students have to note down what is at a given grid reference or have to give the grid reference for a specific object or place.
- Play 'Battleships'.

Pie graphs
- Find some examples of pie graphs in books, newspapers etc. Display them and ask for volunteers to explain them. (Sum up by saying that a pie graph is just like a pie cut into wedges or sectors that shows the fraction of a total number.)
- Make a class pie graph. Collect some data based on a current class interest. Turn it into a percentage and place it on a pie graph.

Demonstrate this first then ask students to collect and represent some other information.

Line graphs
- Over the morning collect some statistics from the class every thirty minutes (for example, the number of students sitting down, the room temperature, the number of students not working quietly etc). In front of the class plot this information on a prepared line graph. Ask for some volunteers to 'read' some information from the graph.
- Place students in pairs and ask them to measure the perimeter of different sized squares. Have each pair plot their information on a class graph.
- Extend the line and ask students to predict the perimeter of a square not measured.

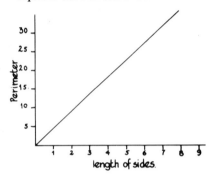

- Plant some wheat on wet cotton wool. Have students measure their wheat's growth each day and plot it on a line graph.

Problem solving
- Students could make a toy by enlarging a pattern using grids.

Length

Awareness of the attribute of length
- Distribute materials, e.g. matchboxes or Unifix cubes. Ask pairs to make a long wall (specify the height). Discussion of terms such as short, long, longer, may develop — these words could be listed on a poster.

Estimation
- Ask students in groups of six or eight to place themselves in order of height. Ask students to estimate, without standing, who will be taller: e.g. Is Sam taller than Beau? How much taller do you think Hannah is than Steele?
- Make a list of small and tall items in nature.
- Cut a hole in the top of a shoe box. Select some items such as a stick, a ruler, a pen. Ask students to guess which one would fit into the hole. This could be an oral or written exercise.

Equality/inequality
- Ask students to find two items in the room that are the same length. You could list or draw these on a large piece of paper.

- Play a game with counters, jelly beans, etc. Give two students a handful each. Ask them and other group members to guess who has more. Then ask the students to share so that they both have an equal amount.
- Read *Something Absolutely Enormous* by Margaret Wild. Hold up a piece of wool for ten seconds then remove the wool from sight. See if they can cut a piece of wool of equal length, then measure it against the original piece of wool.
- Reread *Something Absolutely Enormous*. Ask 'If we each made five squares for the quilt how long do you think it would be?' For example: longer than — our room? — the netball court? etc.
- Have all the children remove their shoes. Select five or six shoes and place them toe to heel in a line. Ask for a volunteer. Using the same number of different shoes ask a volunteer to make a line of the same length?

Comparisons/ordering
- Ask three students to cut a piece of string and hold it in front of themselves. Order them in some way then ask the rest of the group to guess why you chose that sequence. Alternatively, invite several students to stand at the front of the class and sequence them, then jumble them and ask for volunteers to put them back in order.
- Measure a table, blackboard ledge etc. with two different items e.g. chalk, a pencil. Which will you need more of? Students often find this difficult. Try this again with other measuring items.
- Ask students to get together a number of their belongings, e.g. a shoe, a pencil, a jumper, and compare the different sizes. Place them all in groups and order them; e.g., all the pencils, all the shoes, etc.
- Hold up a strip of cardboard. Give students three minutes to find one thing longer and one thing shorter than your cardboard strip. Students must find three things in the room: one longer, one equal to and one shorter than the given unit.
- Have students bring their teddy bears to school. Place them in order from tallest to shortest. Students may think of other ways to order them.
- Collect sticks or leaves outside. In pairs, lay sticks/leaves side by side so that the two rows are equal in length.
- Have students estimate then check which would make a longer line: ten shoes or ten dusters? Try this with other items.

Common units
- How many students' hands would be equal to ten teachers' hands? Have students trace and cut out their own hands to measure and record.

- Guess, then check the length of a person or an object using discrete materials?
- Ask the tallest and shortest child in the class to choose an object in the classroom to measure themselves, (e.g. a duster). Students predict how much taller one is then measure them to check their prediction.
- Each student chooses something to measure with. Give them five minutes to go around the room to find items that are between five to ten times as long as their chosen item.
- Go to the car park. Predict which is the smallest/largest car. Draw lines parallel to each end of the cars. Measure with a chosen item and compare.

Formal units
- Give students strips of paper. Ask them to draw centimetre divisions until they think they have a 30 cm ruler. Check against a ruler. Turn over and make a standard ruler. During this session, or at another time, use this to estimate then measure the length of classroom objects. Check with the home-made ruler.
- Use the meter ruler. Turn it so the class cannot see the numbers. Move your finger or an object along the ruler from 0 to 10, 20, 30, etc. The class guesses how far you have indicated/moved. To more fully involve students ask for a volunteer to run this activity.
- Have students measure part of their body with their home-made rulers. They can record their findings and compare them with a friend.
- Ask students to work in pairs to use their home-made rulers to measure the length of the classroom. They should begin to see the need for a larger unit. Can they think of another way to measure?
- Place Cuisenaire rods on the overhead projector. How many different ways could we use the rods to make a length of 10 cm? Have a 'scribe' record this on a chart for display.
- Using an overhead projector transparency sheet make a 30 cm ruler with centimetres clearly marked. Ask for volunteers to measure an item placed on the overhead projector. Emphasise the importance of starting at '0'.
- Place a large sheet of paper on the board. Each student needs a ruler, pencil and a partner. One student is named the 'ruler', the other is the 'checker'. Give each pair a length, e.g. 15 cm. The 'ruler' rules the length, the 'checker' checks it. Later they can change roles for another length. Get the students to write their initials beside their line and hang the poster around the room. (To make this even more difficult get them to estimate first.)
- How many Smarties does it take to make 20 cm? Ask students to guess first. Place a transparent ruler on the overhead projector to check. Then eat them!

Need for larger units
- Roll a trundle wheel in front of the class and ask the students to tell you what they know about it. Write this on a chart for future reference. If the 1 metre length doesn't come up ask: 'How can we find out how far it is around the wheel?'.
- Guess and measure the width of the basketball court with centi-cubes. Discussion should lead to the need for a larger unit of measure.
- Try this again using paces or a trundle wheel. Have students select areas to measure. Extension discussion could include: 'What fractions of a _____ is the basketball court?'. Calculate the distance around the school.
- Show a variety of objects to the class, for example: a metre ruler, a 30 cm ruler, a trundle wheel, string, paper, etc. Have a number of irregular shapes cut out from cardboard. Ask for suggestions and demonstrations of how these could be measured.
- Choose two points in the school ground, e.g. the classroom door and front gate, or use a map of the school. Ask for suggestions of the best route to take to get from one point to the other. Write them down on a chart and then measure them.
- How many metres long would all the students in our class be if we lay end to end? Guess first, try it, then check.

Need for smaller units
- Have a competition: 'How many things can we fit in a matchbox?'. Come up with a list. Put them in order according to length. Measure them exactly. This will demonstrate the need to use millimetres.
- Make a paper aeroplane using instructions with millimetres.
- Ask children to measure all their fingers. What is the difference between each one, e.g. the little finger and thumb. Are their fingers on the left hand the same as those on their right? They might like to check their toes at another time. Have students use wool and a ruler. Measure the circumference of their thumbs.
- Enlarge a map using an overhead projector or sheet of large paper. Discuss scale. Ask students to draw something to scale, e.g. the classroom. Instead of drawing, some students might like to cut and paste shapes to represent areas in the room.

Fractional units
- Ask students (in pairs) to cut a piece of wool that is one metre long. (You will need a number of rulers or tapes to check.) Then ask them to fold it in:
  $\frac{1}{2}$,
  $\frac{1}{4}$, $\frac{2}{4}$, $\frac{3}{4}$,
  $\frac{1}{3}$
  Measure how many centimetres this is. Students could record and display this information.
- Ask two students to hold a length of rope. Ask another two students to stand between them at equal distances. Walk from one end to the first student. Ask: 'How far along the rope have I

walked?'. Alternatively, place the rope on the floor in the shape of a square or triangle, and ask a volunteer to walk a fraction of the way around the shape, e.g. ⅓, ¾, etc.

- Ask students to find a stick 1½, 1¼, etc. the length of a ruler etc.
- Place the large Cuisenaire rod on the overhead projector. Call this 1 metre. Now place smaller rods beside it and ask the students to describe the fraction and length it represents in centimetres, e.g.

1 m

½ m or 50 cm

Now rename them: e.g. 75 cm = .75 m.

Problem solving
Length/money
Length/time

- Make up an orientation trail using trundle wheels or give students a school map and ask them to design one themselves.
- Make a 3D model (to scale) of the school.
- How much would it cost to make a dress? You need five metres of fabric which costs $8.50 per metre, and a dress pattern which costs $2.50. You also need two buttons that cost 60c each, and cotton that costs 50c.
- Find out the time that it takes to travel certain distances by train, car, etc. For example: if it takes ten hours to travel 1000 km by car, how long would it take to drive from Melbourne to Perth?
- Using milk cartons, construct the Great Wall of China or a bridge. If it takes four cartons to build 50 centimetres, how many will you need to build a wall four metres long? Guess, then build on!
- Roll up lengths of Plasticine to make railway tracks. Which is longer — the curved or straight track?

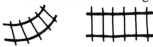

- Can you make your own trundle wheel? Try inventing a new size, e.g. 2 metres.

Money

Recognition of coins

10c	20c

- The class sits in a circle. In the centre place two piles of coins (e.g. 10c and 5c) and two pieces of paper, labelled appropriately for each pile. Two students race to try to be the quickest to sort the coins onto the correct sheet. This can be repeated as often as you wish with different students and coins.

- Hold up a coin for the class to identify; then place it under one of three identical plastic cups. Try the old pea game (juggle the cups around and ask the class to try to identify which cup the coin is under — they must say the name of the coin as they identify which cup it is under). Try this again with different coins.
- You can extend this by graphing one of the turns.

I think it is under		
left	middle	right

- Have volunteers come to the front of the class and place their hands behind their backs. Show the class a coin; the volunteers have to identify the coin by feel only.
- Place any four coins on display. Students have a short period of time to study them to try to remember which coins are there. Cover the coins — students write down the coins they remember. Check the coins again. Repeat this with different combinations or more coins if the students are very confident.

Equivalent values of coins
- Put Blu Tack on the back of some coins then place one (e.g. 10c) on the board. Students take it in turns to use the other coins to make 10 cents in as many ways as possible.

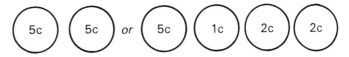

- Make cards to attach to each child (use a piece of paper with a pin or stickers). Write the value of a coin on each label. As you call out the value of a coin, for example 50c, the students get into groups to make that value (this is a good activity to do outside too.)
- Put the students into co-operative groups of six to eight and give each group a large sheet of paper with a money value written on it, e.g.

```
             50c
10c + 10c + 10c + 20c
    20c + 20c + 10c
```

Give the groups five minutes to brainstorm and write down as many ways to make equivalent values to this coin as they can. Share these with the class and display them around the room.

Shopping, money games, buying and selling activities

- Create a shop and use it for drama activities. Ask for volunteers to be the customer and shop keeper. Write out a series of situation cards. Students must tender the most appropriate money and receive the correct change.

> You want to buy 3 combs for 25c each and you have
>
> ($1)   ($2)   and   (50c)

- The shop can also be used for non-directed activities.
- Make a class shopping list for a special lunch. Using advertisements from the newspapers work out the cost of your meal and/or compare prices at different shops.
- Sit the class in a circle and chant 'I went to the supermarket and bought . . .'. Each student takes it in turn to repeat what has already been said and then name an item they could buy that begins with the next letter of the alphabet.
  Make this into a class book with each student doing his/her own page. The students must then find out the price of their own items.
- As a whole class modelling exercise show on the blackboard your calculations of the whole bill from the game above.
- Read *The Shopping Basket* by John Burmingham. Discuss the items Stephen had to buy and compare this story with the students' own shopping stories. What do they think Stephen's shopping would cost? Have students estimate and then perhaps someone could check the prices in the supermarket for their own project.
- Do a quick quiz, e.g.:

> If I had 2m of string and each metre cost $2 how much would it cost altogether?

Equivalent values of $1 and $2

- Play 'Make a dollar, break a dollar'. Each student will need a paper and pencil. Tell them to choose a number between 0 and 50 and write it down; this is how much money they have. Get them to draw this as coins, e.g. 26 becomes 26c:

(20)   (5)   (1)

Have a volunteer roll a large dice; whatever value it shows is the amount of money students receive. They must add this to their current money and represent this using the least number of coins possible. The first student to earn $1 wins.

26c plus 6c = 32c

- Extend this game by aiming at different values such as $2 or $1.50 or by subtracting some rolls of the dice.
- Try playing 'Fortune'. Two volunteers are needed, the object of the game is to gain as much money as possible! See pages 105 and 106 for activity cards. Place them in a box to be drawn out. Place play money in a central bank and give each student $1 to start. Players must always have the smallest possible number of notes and coins and may trade money with the bank to ensure this. For example:

$\boxed{\$2}$ + $\boxed{\$2}$ + $\boxed{\$5}$ + $\boxed{\$1}$ may be traded for $\boxed{\$10}$

Interrelationships between coin and note values

- Quick quiz
  'What is ½ of 50c?'
  'What is ¼ of $1?'
  'What is ⅕ of 50c?'
  etc.
- Cut out advertisements (or ask students to do this) for ten items from the supermarket that cost less than $10 each. Display them and ask for volunteers to stick them onto a chart in order of price.
  Now discuss with the class what fraction of $10 each price is.

ITEM	COST	FRACTION OF $10
bread	$1.00	¹/₁₀ or .10

Interrelationship with the number system

- Enlarge a supermarket check out bill on a photocopier. Ask students to:
  - select any five items and calculate the bill
  - select any five items and deduct the total from $20
  - find out how many items cost less than $1.50
  - choose three items, how much would it cost to buy six of each of them?
  - calculate the cost of a meal.

Interest and percentage

- Ask students to find pictures and prices of a car that they like. Tell the students that for every $200 they spend on it they must pay $5 transfer fee, that's 2½%. Have them use a calculator to work out the total transfer fee.
- Ask students to choose a house in the paper that they would like to buy. Work out the interest to be paid if it was ten, fifteen or twenty per cent.
- Make bankbooks. Write amounts of money on cards (this would vary for different age levels between $100 and $100 000). Use a lucky dip system and treat the cards as credits and debits at various times (see also the game of 'Fortune'). Ask students to calculate their interest at the end of the month.

The story of money
- Write a series of questions, display and discuss them. For example: When was money first used? What are the currencies of different countries? Students could use them as ideas for their projects and then present the information to the class. Ask for volunteers to become the 'money expert' for a certain day.
- On the 14th of February 1966 Australia changed from pounds, shillings and pence to the decimal system of dollars and cents. Have students research this change.
- Ask students to bring money from other countries. Compare the sizes, symbols and values etc.

Problem solving
- Read *A Pet for Mrs Arbuckle* by Gwenda Smyth. Using a map of the world have students map Mrs Arbuckle's progress and then, assuming her journey cost 75c per km, calculate the total cost of her trip. Could students find a better or shorter way for her to have travelled? What would this have cost:
  If it costs
  - $___ per km to travel by train?
  - $___ per km to travel by bus?
  - $___ per kim to travel by plane?
  - $___ per km to travel by ship?
- Have students consider which would be the fastest, safest, cheapest or most comfortable means of transport. As a co-operative group activity have students justify their answer.
- What is the 'ideal holiday'? Co-operative groups agree on a destination, length of time, schedule etc. Using holiday brochures, ask them to calculate the total cost.

Mass

Comparison of two masses by hand
- Prepare the items listed below for students to compare. Place them on a table at the front of the class. First have students predict which will have the greatest mass, then have volunteers lift the objects to test their prediction. Once the students have tested their predictions unwrap each parcel so they can see the contents. Put all the comparisons on a class chart for later discussion.
  - Collect two clear plastic containers of the same size. Fill one with rice and the other with crushed up paper.
  - Wrap a brick and a large empty shoe box in colored but different paper.
  - Wrap an empty matchbox and a shoe box full of small stones.
  - Fill two matchboxes with sand then wrap for comparison.
  - Wrap two more matchboxes, one empty and one filled with sand, gravel or wheat.
- Discuss the chart that has been constructed. Lead the discussion to highlight the following points:

WHICH HAS THE GREATEST MASS?

- rice was heavier than paper
- a brick is heavier than an empty box
etc.

- objects of the same size can have the same mass or a different mass
- a large and small object can have the same mass
- a large object can have greater mass than a small object
- a small object can have a greater mass than a large object.

Hopefully students will initiate these conclusions themselves. They can be recorded on a chart.

- Read *Jim and the Beanstalk* by Raymond Briggs. Ask students to explain which of the two main characters would have had the greatest mass. Are they sure of this? How could they prove it?

Comparison of two masses — see-saw experiences

- Take the class outside and place two students of similar size on the see-saw. Let them ride on it for a few minutes then give one a schoolbag full of books to hold. Ask the class to explain what happened and why. Ask for suggestions as to how they could balance the extra mass.
- Tell the class you would like to have a ride on the see-saw now and put the lightest student on the other end. Why is the student up in the air? What does the class suggest you do about it?
- When you return inside ask the class to use pictures to record what happened on the see-saw. Share their pictures and display them around the room.

Comparison of two masses using the pan balance
One-to-one relationship

- Show the class the pan balance and ask what this reminds them of. Students will probably tell you that it looks like a see-saw. This is the time to refer back to their experience on the see-saw and the pictures they drew about it. Ask 'What happens when we put something heavy on one end of a see-saw?'. 'Will the same thing happen to the pan balance?' Ask a volunteer to check.
- Show a number of objects in pairs:
  - a book and a duster
  - a pen and a rubber
  - a shoe and a sneaker.

  Ask students to predict which will have more mass and then get a volunteer to check the predictions using the pan balance.
- Set pairs of students the task of finding two objects that have the same mass. Tell them they have only five minutes to meet your challenge.
- Place a book on one side of the pan balance, ask five volunteers to find an object that has greater mass than the book and five volunteers to find an object with less. They have one minute to do so and then the class can check their objects using the pan balance.

Other mass relationships

- For the following activities the class will need some way to keep count; you could use a bead frame or have a volunteer keep a tally (for example ||||| ||) on the blackboard.
- Select an interesting toy and place it on one side of the pan balance. Ask for predictions as to how many counters will be needed

to equally balance the pan balance; these could be listed on the board. Now measure and count to see how accurate the predictions were.

- Try the activity above with a variety of objects, for example:
  - how many nails balance a hammer?
  - how many knitting needles balance a large ball of wool?
  - how many pieces of chalk balance a duster?
  - students pose their own problems for their partner.
- Place twenty or thirty counters or clothes pegs in one side of the balance ask the class to see if they can find an object around the room that has the same mass. Set a time limit of perhaps five minutes. (You may need to have three or four balances set up to avoid a long wait for students to test their objects.)
- Divide the class into co-operative groups of four to six students. Give each group two plastic bags containing a number of sorted objects. One group might get one bag of five dusters and another bag containing ten pieces of chalk, for example. They may use any method (except a pan balance or scales) to determine which bag has the greater mass. Have the groups share their findings with the rest of the class.

Comparison and ordering of three masses

- Read the story *The Great Big Enormous Turnip* by Alexei Tolstoy. Ask the class to place the characters in order of their mass. Which character do they think was the most help in pulling out the turnip? Students could break into groups of selected characters to think of reasons to justify their answers.
- Place students into co-operative groups and tell them that they must try to solve the problems you will give them within five minutes. Without using either a pan balance or scales they must first find two similar objects with different mass (for example, two books, two pencil cases or two shoes). Once they have done this they must find a third similar object which has a mass in between the first two objects. Once the group is sure of its results they may test them out using a pan balance. Later have each group present their methods and results to the class during share time.
- Select three clear containers of the same size with different items such as Cornflakes, rice and water. Ask the class to place them in order of their mass. Have a volunteer check this with the pan balance.

Measurement of mass using mixed objects

- Collect a box of mixed objects, such as counters, buttons, pieces of chalk, nuts, bolts or nails etc. Place a book on one pan of the balance. Ask students to predict how many objects from the 'Junk Box' will be needed to balance the book? Ask for a volunteer to test the predictions using the pan balance. Try this again using a variety of other objects from around the room.

- Ask students to volunteer to weigh three books of varying size and place the information on a class chart. Now weigh a fourth, very small book using only the lightest objects from the 'Junk Box'. Discuss the results from the chart. This should lead to students recognising the need for a common unit of measurement.

Measurement of mass using common objects

- Place students in co-operative groups. Give each group a pan balance, a pile of common objects such as counters and five items to weigh. Explain that they have ten minutes to find the mass of each item and record their findings to share with others.
- Repeat the previous activity giving the groups five different items, but this time tell them to place the items in order from heaviest to lightest.

Measuring the difference

- Have the class read the poem 'The Old Woman who Lived in the Shoe'. Now place one of your shoes and a shoe from the smallest-footed member of your class on the pan balance. Ask students to nominate which shoe they think has the greatest mass. The answer is obvious, but then ask for suggestions as to how you could make both sides balance. When the suggestion to add some extra weight is made, have one volunteer add counters while the rest of the class keep count. Add this information to a class chart. Discuss the difference between the weight of the shoes.

THE TEACHER'S SHOE	
Name	How many counters lighter than the teacher's shoe
Sue	24
Peter	15
Salvatore	19
Rebecca	14

- While the class continues with their individual maths activities allow students to work in pairs and find the difference between the mass of their shoe and yours. Add this to the class chart for discussion at the end of the session.
- Place a book and a pair of scissors on the balance. Have a volunteer use counters to measure the difference between these two objects. Ask the class to suggest ways of writing the result in a mathematical way.
- Try this with other pairs of objects and methods of recording. Place these on a chart for display around the room.

Introducing the first formal units

- Collect five plastic supermarket bags and fill them with one kilogram of different objects, such as rice, counters, paper, stones or fabric. Place them on a table, but don't tell the class what they weigh. Let the class vote to place the bags in order of their mass. Now weigh them on a pair of bathroom scales and discuss the results.

- Place students in co-operative groups and give each group one of the kilogram bags. Tell the groups they have ten minutes to find three items around the room that weigh close to one kilogram and then record their findings for display to the rest of the class.
- Give each co-operative group one of the kilogram bags. They must then find three items that weigh approximately one kilogram. One must have a larger shape than their bag, one must be nearly the same size and one item must be smaller. Once again have each group record their results for display and discussion.
- Give co-operative groups of students either a set of bathroom scales or a pan balance and a kilogram weight. Challenge them to finding three items with a total mass of one kilogram.
- Make a SUPER CHALLENGE sign that sets a class problem. Give each student a small slip of paper on which to write their answer and their name. This is then posted into a 'voting box'. Have a volunteer measure out one kilogram of wheat on the pan balance. Read through the students' 'votes' to see who was closest. Congratulate the winner.

The use of scales
- Have the class brainstorm a list of all the types of scales and their uses.
- Do some cooking. It's a great way to practise using scales. Students have a vested interest in measuring accurately if they want to be able to eat what they cook. Cooking can either be done as a whole class activity or in co-operative groups where the recipe and ingredients are given to each group and they are then responsible for their own cooking.
- Ask students to bring a set of scales from home. Test these for accuracy by placing a one kilogram weight on each one. Discuss the results. For example, which tend to be more accurate, bathroom or kitchen scales?
- Ask students to weigh their pets (or borrowed pets) when they go home. This can be done by weighing themselves first then weighing themselves holding their pet. They can then calculate the weight of their pet and record this to present to the class for discussion and comparison the next day.

Need for a smaller unit
- Weigh someone's lunch. Place it on a pan balance. Ask students to estimate how much less than a kilogram it weighs? Use counters to calculate the difference.

- Now weigh a variety of objects from around the room to see how much less than a kilogram they weigh using counters and mixed objects to calculate the difference. Place this information on a chart for discussion. Students should come to recognise the need for a smaller standard unit.

Parts of a kilogram

- Place a 2 litre milk carton filled with 1 kilogram of rice on one side of the pan balance. Show the class a variety of standard weights (such as 200 g, 250 g, and 500 g etc.). Ask volunteers to try to find two weights that will balance the kilogram weight and record this on a chart. Repeat the procedure using different numbers of weights.

Parts of a kilogram

- In co-operative groups set students the challenge of finding three items that weigh approximately ½ a kilogram and three items that weigh ¼ of a kilogram. Have them record their results to present to class.
- Give co-operative groups a one kilogram ball of plasticine or playdough and ask them to break it into specific smaller units such as 200 g, 250 g or 500 g. Ask them to record how many of these it take to make one kilogram in a number sentence.

Your group had to make one kilograme of plasticine into 200 gram ball it took 5 balls to do it.

- Combine this information on a class chart to demonstrate fractions of a kilogram.

1 tonne = 1000 KG
1 kilogram = 1000 G
½ kilogram = 500 G
¼ kilogram = 250 G

Introduction to the gram

- Give each co-operative group a different number of centimeter cubes varying between 5 and 50 and a pan balance. Ask each group to find an object that weighs approximately the same as the counters given.
- In co-operative groups give students a stick made from ten centimeter cubes and another object from around the room. Ask them to find the difference in weight between the two items. Remind them to record both their results and the way they went about solving the problem for discussion later.

The gram • Place a 50 g weight on the pan balance and ask students to estimate how many centimetre cubes will be needed to balance the weight. Let the class count the cubes as they are placed on the other pan by a volunteer.

• Try this again with other weights such as 10 g, 20 g and 25 g. Record the results on the board and ask students if they see any pattern emerging.

Problem solving • Show a picture of a see-saw with the heavier person up in the air. Ask co-operative groups to make a list of reasons to explain how this could happen (for example: 'This picture is of an underwater see-saw'. 'The fat man is a blow-up doll.' 'The wind was very strong on that day.'

• How many grains of rice in 1 kg? Find the mass of a grain of rice then pose another question.

• What is the average mass of the students in the class?

• Research the terms 'tare' and 'gross weight' as used on trucks and buses.

• Find the mass of the bricks in a school wall.

• Weigh a telephone book. What is the mass of one page?

• Construct an instrument to measure mass then use it to measure a variety of objects.

Computation

• •

There is a multitude of material available to teach specific skills involved in computation. We have provided some ideas for games and problem solving which teach computation skills in an integrated and enjoyable way.

The operations addition and subtration, and multiplication and division, have been grouped together because they are interrelated concepts. Many of the ideas listed can easily be adapted for other processes.

ADDITION AND SUBTRACTION

Grouping • Play 'Magic Numbers'.
Specify a Magic Number, say 10 or 20, and give pairs of students a dice and a pile of counters. Students take it in turn to roll the dice and collect the number of counters indicated until they reach the magic number. For addition start at 0 and try to reach the magic number; for subtraction start at the magic number and try to reach 0 by subtracting the amount rolled on the dice. The first to reach the magic number (or 0 as the case may be) is the winner. Ask students to verbalise what they are doing as they play. For example: 'I've got three counters and I rolled 4, so now I've got seven counters.'

- Play any board game that requires moving positions as a result of a dice throw, such as 'Snakes and Ladders'. Players move forward the total value thrown on two dice. To introduce subtraction have players move forward on their first throw and backwards on their second.

Recording with numeral cards

- Set up a collection of skittles. Have students take turns to roll a ball at the skittles and record their strikes with numeral cards. For addition they can add up the total number of skittles they knock down, for subtraction take the number knocked down from the total number of skittles. (Provide counters or calculators to help students with their calculations.)
- Play 'Snake's Eyes'. Draw a snake on a long piece of cardboard and cut it into ten equal pieces. On the back of each piece write the numbers 1 to 10 in order so that when the numbers are placed in sequence the snake is correctly constructed on the back. Place the cards on a ledge with the numbers showing in order. Have a volunteer spin a number wheel then turn over the number shown. If the number is already turned over, e.g. 8, a combination of numbers that adds up to 8 (4 + 4; 3 + 5) or, using subtraction, equals 8 (10 − 2) may be turned over. Can the class turn all the snake over or do the 'Snake's Eyes' win?

Introduction of symbols

- Play dominoes. As the students play have them record the total number of the two sets of spots on each domino turned over using numeral and operation cards.

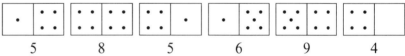

- For subtraction have students deduct the value of each third move. For example:

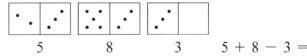

$$5 + 8 - 3 =$$

- Play 'Hookey'. Ask players to record their scores with numeral and operation cards. Introduce subtraction by having students add their first two scores and then deduct every third.
- Make equation cards, e.g. $5 - 2 = 3$ $4 - 1 = 5$ for small groups to act out. For example $5 - 2 = 3$: A group of five students line up together, two move away to leave three. The rest of the class is then asked to guess the equation. Have the audience record their guesses.

Reading and writing equations

- Ask groups of students to make their own equation cards to act out using the answers recorded in the game above.

Making equations
- Give an answer and ask students to write the question. For example, 'Ten is the answer, what is the question?' Or have students work in small groups for more difficult problems such as 'Use subtraction to decide the question when 345 is the answer.'

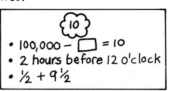

  Ask students to use more than one operation in each equation.
- Draw a clock face on the floor in chalk. Students take turns to stand blindfolded in the centre. They must turn around stopping at a number at random then create an equation using this number as the answer. This can be made more difficult by making the numbers more complex.
- To play this game pairs of students will need twenty counters or they could use a calculator: players take turns to take away between one and five counters (or numbers on the calculator) until all counters are removed. The last player to make a move is the winner. Have students record their moves as equations. By starting at 0 and working towards 20 this game can be adapted to addition.

Complex equations without re-grouping
- Divide the class into co-operative groups and give each group a number of counters. Ask them to come up with a list of ways to regroup them. A recorder can be chosen to keep a record of the group's ideas. Ask them to record calculations as equations using addition and subtraction (for example $27 + 23 = 50; 50 - 23 = 27$). These can be shared with the whole class.
- Ask students to work in co-operative groups. Give each group of students a small square of card onto which they must write any one number between 10 and 100. The groups then place their numbers in random order in a line. Each group must then make a number story or equations about the numbers as they appear in pairs for example:

> - 23 is 24 less than 47
> - $47 - 12 = 35$
> - $12 + 86 = 98$
> - 98 students went jogging but 77 got tired and stopped so only 21 got to the end
> - 21 is much smaller than 53

Have the groups share their equations with the class.

Equations with re-grouping
- Give groups a large bundle of icy-pole or match sticks. Ask them to work out the quickest way to calculate the total number of sticks. They will probably suggest bundling them into groups of 10 (have elastic bands available). Ask them to record their results as either or both addition or subtraction.

Number facts
- Play a number of games to revise number facts and mental computation (such as 'Bingo' or 'Naughts and Crosses') or have a quick quiz (try using a train timetable). Include 'rounding off' in these activities.
- Have students work in pairs. Each student writes down a number between 1 and 10. They then take it in turns to add their number to their partner's number to reach a target number, say 50 or 200. For example: if the numbers chosen were 4 and 6 the game would go:

  4 (+6)
  10 (+4)
  14 (+6)
  20 (+4)
  24 (and so on).

  The winner is the player whose addition takes the total to or over the target number. This game can be adapted to subtraction by starting at the target number and subtracting until the first player reaches 0.

Estimation
- Use the money collected for fund raising or an excursion on one day to estimate the total to be collected over a number of days.
- If there are eighty-two wombats and a number of emus at a sanctuary and there are 200 legs altogether how many emus are there?
- Make a shopping list and estimate the total bill. Use sales catalogues to check the cost of items on a shopping list.
- For subtraction allow a specific budget and ask students to show the calculations as they take the cost of each item away from their budget total.
- Guess the difference in cost between two specific cars or houses. Use newspapers to work out the difference in cost. With cars, find two similar features, for example air conditioning; with houses, find two in one area.

MULTIPLICATION AND DIVISION

Grouping
- Take the class outside for a game. Hold up numeral cards, for example $\boxed{5}$. The students must form groups of that number.

Anyone who is left over is out. Have the class calculate the total. For example, 'If we have six groups of five then we must have thirty altogether.' Alternatively, 'Thirty kids divided into six groups mean there's five kids in each group.' Students could represent this visually.

- Read the book *The Doorbell Rang* by Pat Hutchins. In pairs or small groups ask students to calculate how many cookies each child will get when Grandma arrives. Conversely, if there are twelve children how many cookies will Grandma need to bring for each child to get six cookies? Cut out paper biscuits and make a 'big book' to explain the cookie distribution.

Recording with numeral cards
- Give each student an old calendar sheet to cut up so they will each have one set of numbers from 1 to 30. Give each student an envelope to keep their numbers in. Place containers of counters on the floor and hold up a 'Special Number' such as $\boxed{4}$. Students must make as many groups of four as they can in one minute, they then use their number cards to label their number of groups. Ask questions such as:
  - 'How many groups of four did you make?'
  - 'How many counters do you have altogether?'

  Repeat this with other numbers.
- Play 'Secret Box'. Fill a small box with a large number of small items, for example forty-eight beads. Tell the class that in their spare time they can count the number of beads in the box and then work out how many groups of four there are. Ask them to write their answer on a slip of paper along with their name and place it in a 'voting' box. Explain that before the next maths session you will check the answers to the questions to see how many solved the problem.

Introduction of symbols
- See addition and subtraction for drama equation cards. Adapt this activity to multiplication and division.
- In small groups use a deck of playing cards to play the following games:
  - The dealer deals two cards (e.g. 2 and 5). The player must record the answer to the multiplication sum 2×5.
  - The dealer deals 1 card (e.g. 8) and the player must record a division sum that equals 8 (e.g. $16 \div 2 = 8$).

Reading and writing equations
- Write a group of numbers on the blackboard that multiply exactly. Have students use calculators to work out which numbers go together as multiplication and division sums. (Answer: $9 \times 13 = 117$ or $117 \div 13 = 9$ etc.)

- Students will need paper, pencils and counters or calculators. Roll two large dice. The students must use the numbers rolled to make multiplication or division equations.

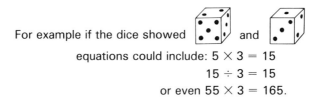

For example if the dice showed [dice] and [dice]
equations could include: 5 × 3 = 15
15 ÷ 3 = 15
or even 55 × 3 = 165.

Students will come up with some remarkable variations given the encouragement.

Making equations
- Give students some operation cards $\boxed{\times}$ $\boxed{\div}$ $\boxed{-}$ $\boxed{+}$. Ask students to use their 'calendar' numeral cards (see page 88) to make equations for a partner to solve.
- Using multiplication and division, ask students to set problems for others to solve. For example, if it costs $200 per term for each student to go to school how much would it cost for two students to attend for one year?

Complex equations without re-grouping
- Play 'Lost Signs'. Write a number of equations on the board such as 88 ☐ 11 = 8 or 5 ☐ 4 ☐ 20. Let students use counters or calculators to find the operation signs that belong in each equation. If you are using calculators you can try more complex problems such as 195 = 15 ☐ 13.

Equations with re-grouping
- Work out whether a larger number divided by a smaller number is greater than the smaller number divided by the larger number.
- Find out the cost of individual items to make a sandwich, then calculate the cost for a family for one lunch, or for lunches for a week or the whole class for a week.
- Read *Anno's Mysterious Multiplying Jar* by Mitsumasa and Masaichiro Anno. In co-operative groups ask students to work out how many items are on each page (a calculator may be helpful).

Number facts
- Give each student a sheet of paper folded in half. Tell the class they have five minutes to write all the multiplication equations they can with the answer of a specific number, for example 144. They must then use the bottom half of the paper to re-write each equation as a division sum.
- Give each student a number from 1 to 12. This is their base number. Hold up a card with another number. Each student must multiply their number by the number you hold up, writing it as an equation. Repeat this activity a number of times holding up different numbers for the students to multiply by their base

number. Ask students to correct a partner's work. This can be adapted for division by giving out only those base numbers that will divide equally into the numbers you hold up.

● See **addition** and **subtraction** and adapt the ideas suggested.

Estimation
● Distribute a dotted grid to pairs of students. The aim of the game is to try to circle all the dots. They do this by grouping any odd number (but only one) between 3 and 11. For example, if they choose 5 they must circle only groups of 5 each time. These must be in straight lines and each dot can only be circled once. (Answer: 7 divides 26 times.)

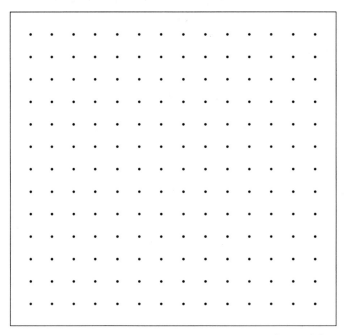

Ask students to design a similar pattern for a friend.

MY MATHS PROJECTS

Name

Date	Activity	Conference

REPRODUCIBLE PAGE

MATHS PROJECT REPORT

Name ______________________

Project/topic ______________________

1 What I/we did

____

____

____

2 What I/we used to help me/us

____

____

____

3 What I/we learnt

____

____

____

4 Other comments

____

____

____

5 Some ideas for others investigating this topic

____

____

____

REPRODUCIBLE PAGE

GROUP ASSESSMENT RECORD SHEET

Names ______________________________

____

Project/topic

____

1 Things that helped us work together:

____

____

____

____

2 Things that we could improve next time:

____

____

____

____

3 Things that we learnt:

____

____

____

____

RECORD SHEET — COUNTING

	Date
To at least 35 Count by one Count in groups — 2, 3, 4 Count backwards by ones Count a group of objects Count to find a position Count using ordinal names Count from different starting points Recognise numerals from 0 to 20 Write numerals 0 to 10	

Make models of numbers to 35
To 10, then 20 . . . 35
  • use materials
  • orally
  • record with numeral cards	

Addition
Subtraction
Comparison of groups
Multiplication
Division
  • sharing
  • how many groups
Calculator computation	

Sort Attribute activities	

REPRODUCIBLE PAGE

RECORD SHEET — COUNTING CONTINUED

Informal use of half and quarter	
Match a pattern Continue a pattern Create a pattern Order groups of object	

Awareness of the attribute of length
Early estimation experiences
Awareness of edges and boundaries
Awareness of area
Awareness of capacity of containers
Awareness of mass
Comparison of two masses by:
  • hand
  • see-saw
  • pan balance
Recognition of coins
Sequence
Names of days
Time cycles	

Comparison through drawing and modelling Pictorial and concrete comparison	
Shapes Language of location	

CO-OPERATIVE LEARNING SKILLS CHECKLIST

Task Skills
staying on task
finishing task
following directions
recording ideas
staying in groups
sharing materials
watching time

Work Skills
self motivated
independent
enthusiastic participant
willing to take risks
creative thinking
logical thinking
displays confidence

Social Skills
listening to others
using quiet voices
taking turns
using names
asking questions
sharing ideas
justifying ideas
reporting ideas
asking for help
helping others
critical thinking
achieving group consensus

(in Wilson and Egeberg *Cooperative Challenges*)

....

PROBLEM-SOLVING STRATEGIES: A CHECKLIST

Clear understanding of the problem
- Restating question
- Identifying integral parts of the problem

Selecting strategies
- Selecting and use of appropriate procedure/resources
- Planning

Collection of information
- Collecting and organising information
- Exploring systematically
- Representing data
  - lists
  - diagrams
  - charts
  - graphs
- Trial and error
- Recording approximations
- Summarising information

Finding patterns and eliminating options
- Looking for patterns
- Generalising
- Identifying and eliminating alternatives
- Verifying reasonableness of answer
- Working backwards

Presenting and justifying conclusions
- Symbolisation
- Communicating ideas
- Presenting clearly

Note: Stages are not mutually exclusive.
(in Wilson and Egeberg *Cooperative Challenges*)

REPRODUCIBLE PAGE

PAIRS OF SHAPES

THE QUILT GAME

Instructions

- Photocopy this page and the next. Cut out the quilt pattern, the quilt squares and the rules. Glue the rules to the back of the pattern and cover it with Contact or place it in a plastic sleeve.

Rules

- Two players may play at a time.
- Method One — Take it in turns to put down one, two or three squares at a time. Whoever puts down the last square wins.
- Method Two — Take it in turns to roll a dice. Players put down as many squares as there are dots on the dice. Once again, whoever puts down the last square wins.

<table>
<tr><td></td><td></td><td></td><td></td><td></td><td></td></tr>
<tr><td></td><td></td><td></td><td></td><td></td><td></td></tr>
<tr><td></td><td></td><td></td><td></td><td></td><td></td></tr>
</table>

THE QUILT GAME CONTINUED

Quilting squares for the quilting game

R E P R O D U C I B L E   P A G E

PERIMETER GAME

Enlarge this sheet on the photocopier. Stick it on cardboard and cover it with contact or place it in a plastic pocket.

Rules

Two people may play this game. Place your counters on either the squares or the circles. Throw the dice to move your counters around the perimeter of the shape in any direction. The first person to have their counters on the other person's shape wins.

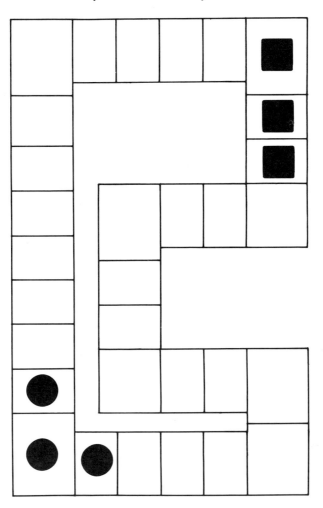

CLOCKLOTTO

MAZE

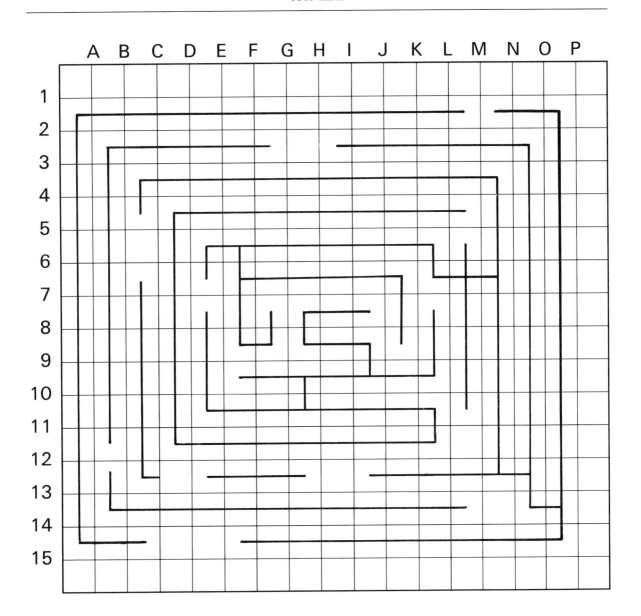

Instructions
• Mark the co-ordinates given below on the grid with small crosses.
• Solve the maze by ruling lines to join the crosses.
Start 1M, 2M, 2A, 12A, 12B, 6B, 6C, 4C, 4M, 5M, 5D, 7D, 7E, 9E, 9G, 7G, 7J, 9J, 9K, 7K, 7L, 12L, 12H, 13H, 13N, 14N, 14E, 15E, Finish.

FIND HOME

Can you work out the grid references to help 😊 get home?

FORTUNE CARDS

You lend your friend your last 10c.

You donate 25c to charity.

You spend 40c at the pinball parlor.

You pay a walk-a-thon sponsorship of 80c.

On the way home you find $2.00.

You lost 32c in the playground.

Your dog swallowed 5c.

You get 54c pocket money.

You spend 11c in the milkbar.

You find 40c in your schoolbag.

You bank 50c.

FORTUNE CARDS CONTINUED

Your mother told you to clean up your room but you didn't and now you can't find any of your money at all.

Grandma gives you $5.00 and says 'Don't spend it all at once.'

You find 50c under your bed.

Your parents give you an extra 20c in your pocket money this week.

You get payed $2.00 for mowing the lawns.

Your sister borrows 20c without asking.

Mum cleans out her purse and gives you all her spare change; that's 93c!

You wash dad's car and he pays you $3.00.

Bibliography

Children's books

Allen, P. *Mr Archimedes' Bath*. Harper Collins, 1985.

Allen, P. *Who Sank the Boat?* Putnam, 1985.

Andersen, H. C. *The Princess and the Pea* (traditional).

Anno, M. *All in a Day*. Putnam, 1990.

Anno, M. and Anno, M. *Anno's Mysterious Multiplying Jar*. Putnam, 1983.

Blakely, P. *Anna's Day*. Black, 1973.

Briggs, R. *Jim and the Beanstalk*. Putnam, 1989.

Burnigham, J. *The Shopping Basket*. Harper Collins, 1980.

Carle, E. *The Very Hungry Caterpillar*. Putnam, 1986.

Comber, B. *Dad's Diet*. Bookshelf (Martin), 1987.

Furchgott, T. and Dawson, L. *Phoebe and the Hot Water Bottle*. Harper Collins, 1980.

Gretz, S. *Teddy Bears Go Shopping*. MacMillan, 1984.

Hill, E. *Where's Spot?* Putnam, 1980.

Hinchcliffe, J. *Hilton Hen House*. Ashton Scholastic, 1987.

Hutchins, P. *Don't Forget the Bacon*. Morrow, 1989.

Hutchins, P. *The Doorbell Rang*. Greenwillow, 1986.

Jonas, A. *The Quilt*. Greenwillow, 1984.

Milne, A. A. *Now We Are Six*. Dutton Child Books, 1988.

Roenffeldt, R. *Tidalick the Frog who Caused a Flood*. Puffin, 1980.

Smyth, G. *A Pet for Mrs Arbuckle*. Ashton Scholastic, 1982.

Tolstoy, A. *The Great Big Enormous Turnip*. Heinemann, 1974.

Wild, M. *Something Absolutely Wild*. Ashton Scholastic, 1984.

Wildsmith, B. *All Fall Down*. Oxford University Press, 1987.

Williams, G. *The Chicken Book*. Fontana, 1984.

Reference books

Baker, A. & J. *From Puzzles to Projects*. Nelson, 1988

——*Mathematics in Process*. Heinemann, 1990

Baker, D., Semple, C. & Stead, T. *How Big is the Moon? Whole Maths in Action*. Heinemann, 1990.

Baratta-Lorton, M. *Mathematics Their Way*. Addison-Wesley, 1976.

Curriculum Development Centre. *MCTP (Mathematics Curriculum & Teacher Program)*. Australian Government Publishing Service. 1989, distributed by the National Council of Teachers of Mathematics.

Dalton, J. *Adventures in Thinking*. Nelson, 1986.

Fenby, B., Gibbs, G. & Wilson, J. *Creative Calculating Book 2*. Nelson, 1989.

Gibbs, G. & Wilson, J. *Creative Calculating Book 1*. Nelson, 1989.

Griffiths, R. & Clyne, M. *Books You Can Count On*. Heinemann, 1991.

McKeown, R. *Learning Mathematics: A Program for Classroom Teachers*. Heinemann, 1989.

Victorian Ministry of Education. *Guidelines in Number*. Victorian Government Printing Office (VGPO), 1985.

——*School Curriculum and Organisation Framework*. VGPO, 1988.

——*The Mathematics Framework*. VGPO, 1988.

——*Measurement Curriculum Guide*. VGPO, 1981.

——*RIME (Reality in Mathematics Education)*. VGPO, 1990.

Wilson, J. & Egeberg, P. *Co-operative Challenges*. Nelson, 1990.

Computer Program

Ant Farm. Sunburst Communications Incorporated, 1987.

Authors' Acknowledgements

We would like to thank these teachers, and their students, for their assistance, support and for sharing their work with us:
Greenbrook Primary School — Marg Smith, Mary Monoghan, Carmela Bianco, Andrew Merryweather, Ingrid Wilson, Delys Murray and Ruth Blair.
Eltham East Primary School — Terri Lee.
Lalor Primary School — Andrea Johnson.
Wattle Glen Primary School — Diane Craig.
St Andrew's Primary School — Lana Wilde, Robyn Jones, Paul Stevens and Jenny Foster.

We would also like to thank Yvonne Cahill, Stephen Thorp, Linda Dunn, Mathew Belot, Katie Belot, Daniel Hoyne, Nicholas Lee and Alexandra Lee.